P9-CDI-813

Developing a Christian Mind

a fearless, happy ease amid
the conflicts of secular thought

Nancy B. Barcus

InterVarsity Press
Downers Grove
Illinois 60515

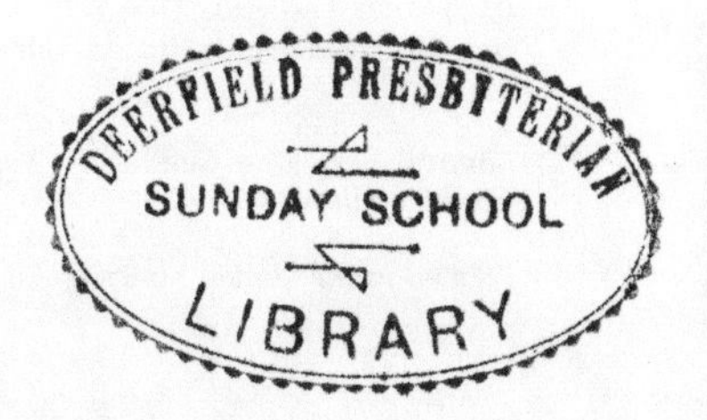

Second printing, November 1979

InterVarsity Press is the book-publishing
division of Inter-Varsity
Christian Fellowship, a student movement
active on campus at hundreds
of universities, colleges and schools of
nursing. For information about
local and regional activities, write
IVCF, 233 Langdon St., Madison, WI 53703.

Distributed in Canada by InterVarsity
Press, 1875 Leslie St., Unit 10,
Don Mills, Ontario M3B 2M5, Canada.

ISBN 0-87784-732-0
Library of Congress Catalog
Card Number: 78-51642

Printed in the United States of America

Dedicated to each one
who encouraged and
joined me in the ongoing quest
for a Christian mind,
especially
James

Preface

"You just haven't thought your position through very well. I'll bet you're one of those Christians!"

Thought and faith are incompatible, we are told—especially faith of the Christian kind, encumbered with its theological creeds. The sooner we can clear our minds of such convictions, the sooner we will be able to think.

Under these pressures, are we better off to disappear and think our thoughts only to ourselves? Certainly it is painful to withstand the stresses of the intellectual marketplace. But Christians, enamored as they are with an absolute God, are sorely needed there. Otherwise, the intellectual spectrum will be skewed. Without Christian thinkers much will be left unsaid, for there is no one else to say it. Tempered by humility and reserved judgment, and confident that God understands all truth even when we are baffled, Christians must "go into all the world." For the world of exploding knowledge and catapulting discovery needs our contribution.

This book is about an attitude, an approach, a fearless, happy ease amid the conflicts of secular thought. I hope the keen-minded reader will find an outlook here that will make believing and thinking a compatible and joyful pair. I do not offer a comprehensive framework, a systematic philosophy or a pocket formula for countering the contemporary philodoctrinal disasters of secular thought. Others have done this. Rather, I propose a quest here: a quest toward the renewal of the Christian mind.

In the first chapter I discuss an approach of openness,

without suggesting that we must embrace other systems or world views. In the middle three chapters I apply this approach to three of today's most prominent territories of thought— science, nature and humanism.

I consider certain key spokesmen in each discussion not to give a comprehensive survey but to represent the kinds of problems and issues now current. These thinkers represent a wide range of interests and convictions. Some apparently have ideas more compatible with Christian convictions than others; some are more overtly attractive than the rest. But each is heard and praised for contributions to the world of thought or for helping us see some things more clearly than we have before. As a result I hope my readers will try other equally heady thinkers, as the questions raised here prompt them to travel other roads.

My concluding chapter deals with the reward and the pain of going on such journeys. There are risks and hardships to be endured. All is not glory on the road to light.

In the midst of what some are calling The Knowledge Explosion, we find that the questions at hand seem ever more difficult, the complexities of life ever more bewildering. Yet this is the time to take courage, to rally our intellectual and spiritual resources, to stay in the arena. It is an exciting age, a disturbing age.

If we learn anything from it, we will at least learn to exchange our triteness and our haste in "settling" complex issues for biblical humility. And if we persevere, enlarged understanding is sure to follow hard upon that better-learned humility of mind. "Make every effort to supplement your faith with virtue, and virtue with knowledge, and knowledge with self-control, and self-control with steadfastness, and steadfastness with godliness, and godliness with brotherly affection, and brotherly affection with love" (2 Pet. 1:5-7). Knowledge is not an isolated or an unchristian part of the world. It is part of the very fabric of what it means to be a Christian. It is not separate from such virtues as humility and love. We have the truth and yet we do not know everything. So we are humble. We speak the truth as Christ would speak, in love, because we are speaking to people.

Enlarged understanding, humility, love. How we need them! In fact, they were to be the hallmarks of that first creature God created in his image. The moment challenges us. It is time to reclaim, to exercise, the heritage of the Christian mind.

The Christian Mind: Introduction

1

Indeed it all began in the Garden of Eden. An ancient argument says that the uninitiated, the common people ought to leave heady intellectual matters to the caretakers of literature and theology and not bother their pretty little heads about such things. So said some of the Fathers, adding that as Adam and Eve were deceived by the promise of the Tree of Knowledge, you will be too.

Well, true. Adam and Eve should never have eaten that fruit. Of course they should never have disobeyed God by grabbing rashly for knowledge. Indisputable. But can the argument of the Fall be stretched to suggest that knowledge is a close cousin of the sin of disobedience, an easy tool of the Tempter? Should knowledge be disregarded altogether? Or is it possible to understand that God intended to make knowledge accessible in his own, better way?

Where the Danger Lies

Questers after knowledge have had a hard time of it ever since Adam and Eve picked the fruit out of turn. But isn't the moral that they should have waited? If only they had waited! Haste, not knowledge, was their downfall. Love of autonomy, not of philosophy, their fault.

Well, then, is knowledge dangerous? No more so than ignorance. For foolhardy, ignorant people are dangerous. Snapjudgers are dangerous. Rash pronouncers are dangerous. Constricted intellects are dangerous. Oversimplifiers are dangerous. Proud philosophers are dangerous. Rebellious inquirers are dangerous. In all of these it is not the knowledge but the thinker that is dangerous; not philosophy, nor inquiry, but people. The Tree of Knowledge was, after all, God's idea. Reading, discovery, reconsideration can, therefore, become a kind of adventure.

What, then, of that spirit of fear which thwarts our quest? How can we keep from being intimidated by the impossibility of weighing the words of the learned and the esteemed? A passion for "correctness" in Christian circles has instilled this hesitation. True, such fear can mean an admirable humility, a recognition of the complexity of life. But the habitual fear of error, the fear of violating sacred formulas, promotes an atmosphere of distrust and suspicion, a sense that one is treading on unholy and forbidden ground.

Fear can also cause those who insist on pressing ahead to rely on simple formula tests, quickly and easily applied. The result is oversimplification, imitative thinking, and a loss of insight and mental breadth. The discovery process is blunted. There must be another way.

The way of openness gives every claim a hearing, every advocate an opportunity to plead his case in its entirety before beginning the task of judgment. It refuses to measure a thinker's words by any preconceived formula while he is still speaking, because that kind of listening is no listening at all.

This openness does not imply "embracing." It is merely sensing what a speaker earnestly means by the words he uses. It is listening with sensitivity. And we can only listen with sensitivity if we are very slow to apply formulas.

Yet isn't it especially threatening to enter the arena without a formula, without any guide at all? Indeed it is. But the rigid formula is not the only mental equipment available.

Not Wings but Weights

When we confront a new book, a new idea, an unknown but challenging person, what should be our attitude? How should we approach our study of alien thought?

Our primary goal should be to get a clear view of the philosophy or the religion or the ideas in question. As already observed, the key danger is haste. So the first step is to stand back and take a long, clear look. Then perhaps list the issues to be sure you aren't missing something. Then take another long look . . . slowly. As Sir Francis Bacon advised some two hundred years ago, "The understanding must not be supplied with wings, but rather hung with weights to keep it from leaping and flying." The essence of careful thought is to proceed slowly.

"Not very glamorous," you say. No, and I suppose that's what Adam and Eve thought about God's command to wait, compared to the serpent's offer. Obedience and waiting are not particularly glamorous. They require work and struggle and hardship. If we are to be mature in our understanding, as well as in all areas of life, this is what will be expected of us. Christ did not promise things would be easy. "Enter by the narrow gate; for the gate is wide and the way is easy, that leads to destruction, and those who enter by it are many. For the gate is narrow and the way is hard, that leads to life, and those who find it are few" (Mt. 7:13-14).

Armed and sobered by this, we continue our careful inquiry. We must next learn the background of the person proposing the position we are considering. We should be willing to listen to information from someone who is qualified. This qualification includes background, training and recognition by others that this thinker is an authority in the area.

Nevertheless, when an authority in one field moves over into another area, not his own, and continues to speak with the same authority, we may be wary—and rightfully so. Expertise in matters of science does not insure expertise in matters of theology, for instance. Someone learned in one area deserves respect for that learning. This authority does not, however, automatically give him the same authority to make ethical or philosophical judgments about the entire nature of man, the universe, God.

What is at stake here is interpretation. Specialized information moves easily into interpretation in the hands of any human, expert or otherwise. Every person is a philosopher. Hence we need to look beyond the "cold facts" for personal interpretation. Facts rarely, if ever, exist in isolation. They "mean something" to each person who touches them. Not that there aren't well accepted facts like, "the earth revolves around the sun." But even that fact once meant something intensely theological and very disturbing to another generation, and may again, sometime, to still another generation. Today many feel perfectly secure with that fact and have learned to live with even more startling astronomical discoveries.

But the "facts" of each discovery often mean something so important to their discoverer that these personal responses bear implications far beyond the actual data. Indeed those meanings, those interpretations of the data, may make us tremble. At such times we need to clearly separate the data which a thinker offers from the meaning its discoverer has tied to it. Perhaps the data will endure and the meaning will not. Very probably the meaning of the data will change. Information and meaning must be separated. That is the most crucial key to the art of reading and thinking.

A second, crucial point follows close behind. We must understand that all authorities are human beings like ourselves, subject to the same weaknesses. Thus, as soon as possible we should recognize the sound of the voice speaking. Not only must we hear *what* is being said, but *how* it is being said. A slight shift in tone or emphasis can change everything. We need a sharp ear and the ability to watch or to listen for the raised eyebrow, the ironic laugh, the frown that says, "I mean it," or the grin that says, "I don't mean a word." Words taken at face value, without an ear for their speaker, are often misunderstood entirely.

Sometimes we may detect an air of assurance so totally

serious that it is disarming. That very sound of self-assurance should put a person on guard. Is there room for any attitudes or interpretations other than this one? If the speaker is convinced, and masterful, we will be left with the feeling that there are only two ways to view an issue: the right way and the wrong way, the good way and the foolish way. Giving the impression of fairness and rationality, a thinker may actually be very unfair, suggesting that anyone with a clear mind would reach no other conclusions than these. If you detect such a stance, beware. This is likely to be dangerous ground.

On first hearing, our reaction may be hastily emotional. One is stirred, wants to share the speaker's wisdom, to put off foolishness. Here one must stop, and wait. The old adage holds: Apply weights, not wings. In the morning or in five mornings things rarely sound as convincing. Look again at the facts and check out the implications in the meantime. You may find that time is a balm for clearing the head.

But what of these experts? Surely it is rash to assume you or I can counter the judgments of some as learned as they. No. It is not rash. These experts are people too. They view the world through their own biases and prejudgments. The task is to find out what these biases and prejudgments are. The sooner we understand them, the sooner we hear the voice that is speaking, the sooner it becomes possible to assess the information. Experts are but mortals, too, with human fears and concerns. If we hear them sensitively and sympathetically as our fellow creatures, we will be less intimidated, more perceptive of meaning and intonation, more in tune with personal anguish. It is a good thing to perceive the anguish of another. It increases compassion as well as understanding.

Now and then, of course, will come the persuader who wants to convert by any means. He changes our compassion to intimidation by powerful and threatening ideas. Faith seems eroded. Defenses weakened. But again, beware. It is those very shrill voices, those who loudly insist on their own insights, who signal their own insecurity. It matters too much to them that they be right. Hold back. For those who are well established and secure more often exemplify a marked humility, sensing what they do not know as well as what they do. They do not feel threatened by their limitations and are unafraid of contradiction. Not so with those of the shrill voice. No matter who is speaking, the open but careful listener may refuse to be converted.

That Rigid Orthodoxy

The best approach is *reserved judgment*. When we cannot see around dark, difficult or convincing arguments, reserved judgment serves well. No matter how sure and well-substantiated a position seems at the time, the fact is that even the experts change their minds. Or future experts change the "facts" established by the experts who preceded them. Even Einstein knew there were more than a few things he hadn't resolved.

Today, in some fields, experts are hesitant about making final declarations at all. That is a good stance for all to hold in mind. Things look differently at different times. One of the most interesting aspects of literary study, for instance, is tracing the way a thinker changes and develops over the years. Critics view every writer as a soul-in-transit, not as a static entity. Every thinking person is on a pilgrimage to somewhere. Hence, that person's words are expressions of that journey.

Understanding these things should save everyone from rashly peddling his or her own point of view in return. If Christians turn away and make their own rash pronouncements, we will discover the same faults in ourselves that we have ascribed to others. Enlightened by the gospel, at the same time we recognize the limitations of being rational creatures. We are grateful for revelation, grateful for the redemption of Christ, grateful for our part in a meaningful, eternal history. We have less cause than others to despair. But we know our limitations. Amid a mass of conflicting opinions and uncertainties, we trust God for the outcome and remain cool.

In the meantime, though, we must beware of tying the gospel or our understanding of Scripture to any one intellectual construct. The gospel continues to transcend earth-centered, human-centered, sun-centered, galaxy-centered or culturally-centered schemes, and will always do so. Our interpretations are fragile. God's revelation is not.

This is not to say we should convert to *relativism*: the notion that all truth is relative. Relativism is a rigid, orthodox, narrow faith. Narrower than the narrowest Christianity. Moreover, it is self-contradictory. For it falsifies itself, insisting that one believe in it absolutely. And it laughs heartlessly at those who refuse. It banishes such dissenters to its own barren hell and refuses to hear them. It is not a humane faith, this relativism. Sometimes it is a bully. Sometimes it cajoles. But it is always uncompromising. Those who reject it may, with all the dignity and steadiness in the world, refuse to be converted. The relativist has only made his position *look* simple, rational and obvious. He wants to convince you that he has all the cards.

His arguments sound so good at times that they tempt Christians to abandon the life of the mind. Since there seem at the time to be no better answers, some Christians fear that there are none. They fear to defend the idea of a world constructed by a holy and loving God. The idea of a universe that speaks of and points to a redeemer-God seems embarrassing. The militant relativist hoped that he would force Christians into that corner. Then he could say he was right all along, that "faith" hasn't an intellectual card to play. The truth is, though, that there *are* some cards on the table of faith. Many of them. The relativist doesn't have them all to himself. And Christian thinkers mustn't let things go that way. There is no reason to become the relativist's victim, either through propaganda or through muddled thinking.

In all of this, a kind of slow, careful analysis is crucial. Some of today's thinkers, if they do not share a Christian world view, seem committed to condemning it as a nuisance and a failure. Encountering these, we can stand back and take a long look. We should be able to analyze the most obvious assumptions behind the proffered arguments, point out any unfairness or weaknesses in them, and then, just as important, spend time mending failures whenever the criticisms or insights are fair. If we demand fairness from the critics, those same critics will have to be able to expect apology from us or from the Christian community where either has been foolish or ignorant or unwise. For our goal is always to see more sensitively and sharply than we saw before, to the praise of God. We press on to sift and understand the vast resources which are our heritage in the stunning act of creation.

A demanding task? Yes. But not overwhelming. We need never fear to go on. We claim the bedrock of Scripture, the revelation of Jesus Christ, as we proceed. Within Scripture we find the resources to see us all the way through. We find there adequate resources for maintaining essential faith, godly living, holy worship—everything life requires of us.

> Grace and peace be yours in fullest measure, through the knowledge of God and Jesus our Lord. His divine power has bestowed on us everything that makes for life and true religion, enabling us to know the One who called us by his own splendour and might. Through this might and splendour he has given us his promises, great beyond all price, and through them you may escape the corruption with which lust has infected the world, and come to share in the very being of God. (2 Pet. 1:2-4 NEB)

With such a resource of hope and sanity we can push on to begin the journey.

The Exhilaration of Discovery

Once under way, we will sometimes be exhilarated at something unknown, unseen before, coming into view. The excitement of discovery will make all the puzzling things along the way seem worth their pain. At other times we will feel we are in over our heads. It will help then to know that the wisest heads in the world have struggled with these pangs. The lesson of perseverance will provide the way through.

Usually the exhilaration and the hard things will be mixed together. Most often it will take hard thinking to sort them out. But by meeting the discussions head on, recognizing that every thinker of whatever persuasion has a great deal to offer—both in contributions to new thinking and in hard challenge—Christian thinkers will find themselves becoming creative, thoughtful creatures of God.

The discussions which follow are but a beginning. They both praise and question. They suggest alternatives and counter interpretations. They refuse agnosticism, but glean insights, virtues and discoveries. Before us are those landmark challenges which advance and enlighten the special quest of the Christian thinker.

Meaning and the Shattered Box: Science

2

Science immediately comes to mind for anyone seeking the challenges of contemporary thought. In fact the scientific frame of mind is an entrenched mental habit in the twentieth century. Yet science has long been carrying the seeds of its own obsolescence, and today our tendency to worship the certitudes of science is no longer possible.

The Box That Science Built

What started simply enough as a way of observing the world (by using a telescope, by watching an apple fall) became a testing ground for everything we ever believed about the human race, our destiny and even Almighty God. The scientific method—that way of carefully measuring and seeking order from accumulations of data, predicting future activity as a result of that careful experimentation—is good and useful. But we have overdone our enthusiasm. We have praised the abilities of the Method way out of proportion. We have given it unchecked liberties beyond what it ever asked. And by allowing this to happen we have gotten ourselves into a box.

That box is a problem today. The box which science built for us has burst apart and left us with a handful of fragments.

Before this happened there was a happy, optimistic time when we thought we almost had the whole thing described. The universe was a giant clock, running on time, perfectly calculated and calculable. A law called the "law of cause and effect" led time and again through experiment after experiment to sure and expected conclusions. We had the world in our hands! So we thought.

Somewhere thinking people began to turn up more and more things that didn't fit into the scheme. It began to look a little wobbly. And at last, in the early decades of our own century, enough scientists were beginning to see the enormity of the problem that they began to talk to each other about it, and a few even tried to explain it in ordinary terms—to break the news gently to us. Our comfortable, neat description of the universe was breaking down.

It may be no coincidence that about this same time philosophers began to develop acute cases of what they called "existential nausea." They felt all at sea, all afloat, in a very un-neat, un-planned-looking universe. They decided that their own lives must be meaningless, if there were no larger pattern to fit into anymore. And in despair they gave up the whole search for pattern, rejected the hopes which they had banked in science, and developed their brave new creed of courageous despair.

Science had let them down. Or so it looked. But maybe that was placing the blame at the wrong door. Could science help it if people wanted to make of her a New Religion? Could science help it if some Christians had too hastily thrown away their religious faith on the basis of her evidence? Could science help it if the universe turned out to be so much bigger and more complex than was originally thought? If then, as now, people had only learned to exercise the art of reserved judgment, none of the pangs would have been so severe. The closed system of cause and effect, which many have depended upon for generations, had worked against us. We had placed too much confidence in a method and the center could not hold.

Today, though we still depend daily on that causal law in practical matters, we are coming to see that it has some notable limitations. Many things happen in violation of that law. There is a lot more elasticity in scientific declarations now. If only we could have looked ahead and stayed calm.

For actually this weakening of the closed system can be viewed as wonderful news. Why not a miracle or two? Why not an ascension? A resurrection? A feeding of a multitude? The idea of a fixed universe operating by fixed, unbreakable laws has been supplanted by a more open-ended view.

This age of new science has brought an energetic quest to reconsider all our understandings of the universe. The very ambiguity of the mass of information coming in suggests that this is a big world with no easy "boxy" answers anymore. We are out of the box and into infinite possibility. That can, indeed, suggest infinite meaninglessness; or it can instead suggest an infinitely creative and ingenious God "far beyond all that we ask or think," as one biblical passage reminds us. Perhaps some of the things Christians have held most dear aren't so improbable after all.

If all this can be taken by Christians as a cause for optimism, what is everybody so upset about? People are jumping off bridges and breaking their hearts in anguish over the breakdown. The people who hadn't held out for miracles but had transferred their faith to scientific "certainties," are, indeed, the real losers. Everything they had ever counted on seemed to disappear under their feet all at once.

In a universe traditionally described as made of "units" of "measurable matter," the "matter" at last seems to refuse to obey any laws we want to write for it. Powers of observation available now, far beyond the microscope and the telescope, show new and odd kinds of activity. The chaotic scene minutely visible to the scientific eye appears now to spell out immense personal and philosophical chaos.

"What is man, that the electron is mindful of him?" queries historian Carl Becker in dark and heavy humor. He goes on in severer tones to declare,

> Edit and interpret the conclusions of modern science as tenderly as we like, it is still quite impossible for us to regard man as a child of God for whom the earth was

> created as a temporary habitation. Rather we must regard him as little more than a chance deposit on the surface of the world, carelessly thrown up between two ice ages by the same forces that rust iron and ripen corn. . . .[1]

It is a grim picture, Becker admonishes. "Whirl is King, having deposed Zeus!" he paraphrases Aristophanes. Does modern science confirm that meaninglessness reigns?

Looking at a Hat: Whitehead

A clue to the source of this distress may be found in the book of one of the prophets of the modern scientific age, *Science and the Modern World* by scientist-philosopher Alfred North Whitehead. Written in the 1920s, before the ideas had filtered down very far to lay people, the book is still a good explanation of the drift of much modern scientific thought. Tracing the history of science from medieval to classical to modern times, Whitehead explains how the tools, the questions and the concepts of science have changed. The change Whitehead describes is only now breaking in on general consciousness.

The "new scientific vocabulary" he describes is probably unrecognizable to many who have not dabbled in science for a while. Many scientists themselves are unsure what to call the things they are "looking at." The world seems to be in continuous motion. It won't stand still to be measured! It is in dramatic flux, its confines and limits changing with each new discovery, each new theory. Perhaps, say some, the world is energy and not matter at all. What we have always called an "object" may instead be an "event," a unique unrepeatable concurrence of patterns in one particular moment of time. Thus, when I talk to a physicist about something being as "real as a table," he sees only light waves occurring together at a particular moment in some way known better to him than to me, and cannot say what *real* means or even what a *table* is. His keenly developed powers of observation have shown him something entirely different from what I assumed was there. These gaps between what we have "always thought" and what some theoretical scientists now "see" illustrate the new scientific outlook born of theories like the theory of relativity and the quantum theory.

The main problem is that we are still using the terms and concepts of the "old materialism" handed to us from the seventeenth century or before, and are oblivious to a sudden shift in the idea of the nature of matter. Materialism is still an option, but there are others now. These have been circulating for almost fifty years among the prophets of the new science, but the common person has gone on quite as usual, unaware that the safe notions he counted on were being attacked. Things will never be the same. And while the search goes on, our "scientific vocabulary" becomes more and more hopelessly muddled. Which terms shall we use? And, in fact, what shall we say those terms mean? We are now into an entirely new way of looking at and describing the process of life.

But can it even be "described" anymore, ask some? The modern scientists know how difficult it is to "see" anything at all. Description seems simple only to the uninitiated—me. Scientists want us to understand how endlessly complicated the observation process is: when I see a hat sitting on a table I do not see the whole hat. If anyone else sitting beside me sees the hat, he does not see exactly what I do because his angle of vision is different. If he goes to the back of the hat to see what I have missed, then he still does not see what I do. And a hundred people looking at that hat will not see exactly the same thing. How can we talk about the hat at all? Obviously in our conversation we do. But for the purposes of gathering data about the hat to make some scientifically valid statement, we are faced with quite a problem. Whitehead calls our difficulty the "error of simple location." We have failed to see the complexity of the process of description. We have assumed too much too easily.

Someone might very fairly point out that in spite of the "error of simple location" science has worked better than we might think. Science has done a lot of things "right" too. The history of science bears out the accuracy of many of the early experiments. Observation does work, at least to some extent. We just need to recognize its shortcomings and not exalt it as a god. It is a method with more difficulties than we once saw. But scientists have not really stopped "observing" or even "describing." Perhaps they simply do it with more humility and care.

That humility might be the best fruit of the new scientific outlook. Even the one who observes has his own set of problems, being himself a variable in every experiment. As a perceiver, how can we be sure anyone is entirely accurate? There is simply no guarantee. For by certain tricks one can be "gotten" to perceive, or not to perceive, almost anything, observes Whitehead. The "simple perception" of objects ("I'm sure I saw it. I know that's how it was.") is not at all sure and safe.

So what, then? Must science simply despair and stop all its work? It sounds almost impossible to go on. Of course, nothing at all like that will happen. Science is very busily at work, as always. But we now know, whether we are at work or frozen with despair, that we must be extremely *careful* about what we proclaim for ourselves.

Good News for Whom?

A recent church banner starts with the words, "I will not be tonight what I am this morning." Meant as a challenge, it is also a reflection of the new thinking. What am I? Am I "myself" in some kind of stable formula, or do I altogether elude definition? Am I a "definite" creature, or am I an unstable organism, in continual flux? An unstable organism: that is what much of the new thinking says about each of us.

But Whitehead thinks he is giving us good news. He says the tyranny of the old materialism has held us in bondage too long. There are other things in the human experience which the old way never allowed. Now there is room for discussion of the human personality, of values, of a thing which he calls "concrete experience." Surprisingly he says, "a mere logical contradiction" is no reason to rule out other very important kinds of experience.[2] The old closed science must give way. The new science is open.

At this point, perhaps, things become too uncomfortably "open" for Christians who want to find some real absolute in a world of change. Maybe the Whiteheads have pushed things too far in the other direction. Time will tell. But at least there is room for some very important things that we felt cheated of under the old way, things Whitehead calls "the fundamental intuitions of mankind," the things that find their expression in poetry and in the practice of everyday life. Life is far more than a set of fixed formulas. The question is open now. And there is a whole new range of opinion, from those who hold to the old fixed formulas, to those who say there is nothing we can say anymore, to something more attractively in the middle. While the debate rages, and the opinions change from day to day or from decade to decade, the best thing to do is to wait calmly.

Whitehead's book, written in 1925, is still surprisingly relevant. He warns the overzealous defenders of the old ways not to trust too well in what is *seen*. He insists that one must begin to consider the things that don't fit the formulas. He refuses the old view that anything the old science cannot prove is, therefore, invalid. "The fault, dear Brutus, is not in our stars . . . but in ourselves," says Shakespeare in *Julius Caesar*. The fault in this case is in the old science and not in the things it refused to validate. Its too-mechanical method is weak. It was wrong to exclude "religious sentiments," warns

Whitehead. They are fundamental to the human experience.

All of this sounds like very good news for Christians. Whitehead thinks it is very good news for everybody. But again, if so, why all the despair? Partly because we don't like uncertainty. We would like things to be settled. But partly too because a lot of people rushed headlong to the other extreme. From confident fixity they rushed headlong into total subjectivity. How important to keep the balance!

Whitehead foresaw the danger and he tried to patch it up. He put forward a new theory of objectivism which recognizes both the subjective, and the thing-outside. Both halves of reality matter. We are "inside" our sense experiences, but we know "away from" ourselves, outside and beyond ourselves. We seem to reach beyond ourselves, as part of what it means to be human. This human tendency brings Whitehead face to face with the religious question. He wants, he says, to make room for discussion of the two most important forces in our lives: science and religion. Not either/or. We need the vision of something which stands beyond, behind, within, the passing flux of things. We need that life of the spirit entered in the hope of high adventure. We need the energizing force of love. Without religious vision, he declares, human life is but a flash of occasional enjoyments lighting up a mass of pain and misery.

But if one wants to press him for his definition of the religious vision, for his definition of God, he cannot give one. It is not in Whitehead's methodology to be "specific." God is part of the process. That is all one can say. God is not outside the process, not separate, not knowable in some unique or personal way. He is just "there" somehow, as a principle or theory is assumed to describe something "there."

What does Whitehead do about good and evil, then, if God is part of the process? God serves somehow as a limiting factor to separate good from evil and oversee good as a higher way. Theologically, the specifics are hazy. Still, the point is that here is a scientist of the new breed talking again about such things as God and spiritual value. His religious system is too nebulous, perhaps, but he recognizes the need for the spiritual. Within the modern scientific temper, there is still time for dialogue!

Science without Arrogance: Planck

Whitehead's book, written just at the point when the old physics was giving away to the newer concepts, suggests the increasing complexity of the scientific question. That very complexity has not improved since the writing of the book. If anything the complexity is worse. *Worse* is the wrong word, surely. If God made a complex world, it is about time we were finding it out. But we need to stay cool. For just as Newton's fixed principles once seemed obvious and indisputable, so now these new theories are holding the floor, for a moment. But we must expect that the new theories will change many times. Knowing this creates a healthy atmosphere, as long as no one presses his new claims too far, too soon. We can say, "Oh" or "It might be that way." But the bandwagon approach will no longer do. Time will sift and test and modify every proclamation. So history has taught us. We must live hereafter with the tentative attitude.

In fact, that very humility and tentativeness is ably reflected in the writings of Max Planck, who first proposed the quantum theory. In his much read "The Meaning and Limits of Exact Science," he assures us that science must get rid of its arrogance. It can no longer call itself an "exact" science. "Exact science," he says, has a dangerous weak point—its foundation. Science cannot make pronouncements based on "unerring accuracy."[3] Planck goes on to address the same concepts Whitehead deals with.

He warns against hasty panic. The new world picture does not wipe out the old one, he reassures, but permits it to stand in its entirety—simply adding a new condition to the picture. In fact, life goes on much as usual! The laws of classical mechanics hold up very well in certain given conditions which most of us experience daily. The goals of the newer science should not be feared as destructive and threatening. The new science simply aims at a less naive picture of the world and reality.

When he mentions "higher reality," Planck suddenly and surprisingly begins to talk about "ultimate questions." The real goal of science, he declares, is "metaphysical." There it is again. Science always comes to a wall or a chasm, he notes, and once there we begin to think about a "higher reality." Planck believes that there is another metaphysical reality standing behind the world of science—perhaps not behind it in the sense of space, but behind it all the same; perhaps as within or contained together with it, he speculates. . . . Practical life as well as science tells us this. Obtaining this higher reality becomes for Planck an "inexhaustible source of insatiable thirst." This thirst is common to every true research scientist, he believes. And yet the scientist is stymied at the same time. He can never with his own tools take that last step into the realm of metaphysics he thirsts after. Science must shake off its proud name of "exact" in the face of this unreached, perhaps scientifically unreachable, reality.

Toward his conclusion he admits that this reality is the goal of all scientific endeavor—beckoning in the distance. But in the meantime, he says, the scientist must choose between two alternatives: fearful pessimism (about the potential evil of new nuclear science) or a sense of wonder. Few scientists who have ever viewed nature freshly can escape the sense of wonder which accompanies discovery; so we must "see ourselves as governed all through life by a higher power" whose exact nature "exact" science will never be able to fully define.[4]

Significantly, the religious question persists. Planck seeks the answer to the question of higher reality *within* nature, rather than *apart* from it in a higher revelation. His essay, "Religion and Natural Science," indicates that as a scientist he must begin by ruling out miracles. They must "yield ground step by step before the steady and firm advance of science." They are contradictory to the laws of nature. Curiously, even this statement is dated. As mentioned above, some scientists are viewing the boundaries of nature's laws with far more latitude and seem almost willing to put back miracles. A recent essay names scientist after scientist who has become increasingly fascinated with the study of the "impossible." Study of the occult, spiritism, mind-bending and faith-healing has found its way into the scientific laboratory in surprising measure. Says one eminent cancer researcher, "I have removed the word 'impossible' from my vocabulary."[5] Nothing is *impossible* anymore, even in the laboratory.

Something about God

Still, minus the miracle, Planck manages to believe in a God who existed somehow before humans were on earth, who has held the whole world in "omnipotent hands" since the "beginning of eternity" and who will continue to rule long after the earth has ceased to be. That he comes to those conclusions within his scientific structure is most remarkable.

> The natural scientist recognizes as immediately given nothing but the content of his sense experiences and of the measurements based on them. He starts out from this point, on a road of inductive research, to approach as best he can the supreme and eternally unattainable goal of his quest—God and His world order. Therefore, while both religion and natural science require a belief in God for their activities, to the former He is the starting point, to the latter the goal of every thought process. To the former He is the foundation, to the latter the crown

> of the edifice of every generalized world view.[6]

Science can tell us a lot, says Planck, that will drive us back to the religious question: physical science demands that we recognize the existence of a real world independent from ourselves. We are locked inside ourselves, and our perceptions are quite limited. Nevertheless we cannot help but recognize the reality outside our minds which is really there. And we learn modestly as we realize we are not the center of the universe, but an infinitesimal part of it. At the same time we learn to marvel that we are capable of understanding much about its vast dimensions. As we understand these things, says Planck, we eventually come to accept a God. These "things" which lead us to God are the observations of workable "general laws" or "tendencies": all nature seems to operate according to general laws; our mind reflects the opinion that nature itself is ruled by "purpose." Refraining as the contemporary scientist must do from naming the laws specifically, Planck declares that these things are not figments of our imagination. They are really there—outside ourselves. Planck is convinced of that, and that they are working out some purpose, something constructive rather than destructive.

> But there is another, far broader law, which has the property of giving a specific, unequivocal answer to each and every sensible question concerning the course of a natural process. . . . But what we must regard as the greatest wonder of all, is the fact that the most adequate formulation of this law creates the impression in every unbiased mind that nature is ruled by a rational, purposive will.[7]

We seek religion because we are driven to find out our relation to this "really there" ongoing purpose. We want to know the meaning of it all for our own lives. Through science we can answer many of those basic questions, says Planck. That may take a lifetime or more. But in the meantime we must also learn how to live and act. So, Planck observes, religion helps us immediately with those things; religion and science will never conflict. They will work hand in hand on the immediate questions of how to live, and the bigger question of the meaning of life. Further, the two, religion and science, are on two parallel paths to the same goal; together religion and science can fight the destructive forces of skepticism, dogmatism, disbelief, superstition. Says Planck, the great rallying cry is, "On to God!"[8]

Thus, many religious conclusions are possible *within* science—at least for the person who is earnestly seeking religious truth. This does not mean that every scientist will conclude what he concludes, but Planck firmly believes that every serious scientist must care about the religious question. While many people look to religion for more "definite" answers than his approach provides, Planck holds that science can say "at least this much" about God. In a sense, it is a great deal.

> No matter where and how far we look, nowhere do we find a contradiction between religion and natural science. On the contrary, we find a complete concordance in the very points of decisive importance. Religion and natural science do not exclude each other as many contemporaries of ours would believe or fear; they mutually supplement and condition each other.[9]

In another sense, it is not nearly enough. It is a beginning toward conceptualizing God, but it does not bring us close to him. Planck has severely limited us by making religion at all points subject to the "laws of science." By ruling out miracles and supernatural phenomena and saying that science will not "permit" them, he is limiting his, and our, access to religious truth. We are reminded about Whitehead's criticism of this very thing: "What is a mere logical inconsistency when other considerations seem to point in that direction?" The tyranny of laws is less of a barrier to new ideas now. The range of new data pouring in is far too confusing to reduce to a law. This reversal may push one too extremely in the other direction. But it does suggest that the field is open to the religious question.

The Dark Side of the Data: Monod

Max Planck and Alfred North Whitehead have contributed to the possibility of God in the new scientific framework. As Planck warns,

> It is no wonder that the atheist movement which calls religion an arbitrary delusion invented by power-hungry priests and which has nothing but words of derision for the pious faith in a supreme power above man, is eagerly taking advantage of the progress of scientific knowledge; allegedly in alliance with natural science, the movement continues to spread at an ever quickening pace in its disruptive influence over all nations and classes of mankind. I need not go here into a more detailed discussion of the fact that the victory of atheism would not only destroy the most valuable treasures of our civilization, but—what is even worse—would annihilate the very hope for a better future.[10]

But sadly there is no hard and fast guarantee that all discussions will lead directly to God. Turning to Jacques Monod, a contemporary biologist and author of *Chance and Necessity*, we see the range of choices within science, from theistic scientism to stark atheism.

Monod's book itself is an exciting exposition of the new biological theories coming out of DNA research. He is a highly respected researcher. But the philosophical and religious conclusions he draws from that research are very dark. His is an echo of Becker's "Whirl is King" theme—a vivid example of the bleakness possible in the new scientific outlook. At the end of his work he says our "ancient covenant is in pieces." It is time to grow up to that. We have to face the fact that we are *alone* in the universe. And not only alone (as if that wouldn't be bad enough), but alone in a universe of "unfeeling immensity" out of which we came *only by chance*. And since we came on the scene only by chance, says Monod, we had better give up quickly the idle dreams of having a "destiny." We have no destiny, no purpose, no significance. And therefore no laws, no duty, no morality.[11]

This certainly doesn't sound like the affirmations of a Whitehead or a Planck! Monod is a representative of the pessimism which his brand of interpretation can generate. After research comes interpretation, and interpretation offers a wide spectrum from asserting ultimate order and ethical purpose (as many other eminent scientists in many fields still do) to denial of any meaning whatsoever (as another group of eminent scientists does). The debate is open. As long as one is not taken in by the "authority" of one interpretive voice, the debate should remain open—and to our benefit.

Monod comes to his shattering denial of meaning through a fascinating series of chapters on the structure of biological organisms. He replaces the traditional theory of purposive development with his own theory that development occurs by chance. While the middle chapters of the book will be difficult to follow without some background in biology, it is possible to glean enough sense—with perseverance—to follow the arguments. In each chapter are occasional summary passages which, if followed closely, can help a reader grasp Monod's theory about the structure and nature of life.

Briefly his three basic concepts are: First, living beings must be thought of as "chemical machines." These chemical machines are "organized" along "cyclical pathways," each making up a sequence of reactions. (His explanation corresponds to the DNA theory which sees every function of the human body, and of all life, as the result of an extremely intricate chain or combination of chemical reactions, bound together like the most complex series of telephone systems you have ever seen.) Thus, every living organism constitutes a "coherent and integrated functional unit."

Second, Monod disagrees, however, with other theorists who say that the machine is a "designed" machine. It is not designed, he says. It "makes itself" as it goes along. It is a "self-constructing" machine. The macroscopic and the microscopic structures of living beings are not imposed from the outside by any forces or by any god. Instead, the organism "shapes itself... autonomously" by dint of its own constructive, internal reactions. Thus there is no plan, purpose or outside order which has called forth its present development. Every organism has its *own* genetic decision-making equipment for choosing how it shall develop. Each organism is its own boss.

Third, if some outside pressure is placed on an organism it may alter its growth somewhat—but that is secondary. The initial pressure for growth and change is only from within, along genetic pathways. It takes long periods of time and persistent environmental pressures against an organism for its genetic and internal systems to register any response at all. Thus, Monod sees us as genetically autonomous machines, entirely subject to our genetic equipment. True, we are relatively free of pressure from the environment. But we are really "not free" at all. We are entirely at the service of our genetic wiring systems. We will grow in whatever way our complex internal formulas unfold as they are knit together along our genetic pathways. What one does tomorrow is what the genetic pathways caused one to do. I am not an independent, intellectual or moral being—if Monod is right.

The individual is the result of a giant lottery, the biggest lottery in the universe. The terms *chance* and *necessity* found in the title of the book reflect the basis of Monod's theory. This enormous lottery operates at gigantic speed. Nature draws the numbers by chance on an overwhelming and unpredictable scale. This lottery process is what has "caused" the thing most people call "purpose."

Purpose? No. We just call it that, Monod would say. It is just the results of the lottery, and we stuck that name on it afterward. And once those lottery numbers are drawn, life must obey. That is what *necessity* means. We are bound to obey the lottery choices as they come up. Every change, every new number drawn out enters into the present and becomes a new factor in the next drawing. Every new drawing becomes a part of what already is and changes it in some way. Once drawn, the factor is always there. The whole biosphere is bound to every choice. That is the law of the game. We can call it "purpose" if we like, but Monod would prefer we not. The lottery does not intend anything. It just whirls, so says Monod.

Since Monod believes the lottery has no special plans, all our talk about higher meaning is senseless. We are dreaming. Instead he declares that the probability the lottery had something special in mind does not work out mathematically. In fact, he adds, until the lottery draws the choice, the mathematical probability that such a choice might occur can be said to be *zero*. Indeed, the lottery game seems to work against purpose, not for it.

From the Laboratory to the Pulpit

Thus Monod's genetic research suggests to him only total and unrelenting atheism. All spiritual, animistic or theistic systems will have to "give way" before the "fact" of chance. Monod is sure that science has now "blasted at the root" the possibility of the "old covenant." We must awake at last out of our "millennial" dream, realize our total solitude, become aware that like a gypsy we live on the boundary of an alien world, a world indifferent to our music, to our suffering and to our crimes. Since we are alone, Monod proposes a new and unusual creed of his own.

> A kingdom . . . is within man, where progressively freed both from material constraints and from the deceitful servitudes of animism, he could at last live authentically, protected by institutions which, seeing in him the subject of the kingdom and at the same time its creator, could be designed to serve him in his unique and precious essence.[12]

We must design a new kingdom, commands Monod. We must forget ultimates and ignore the rules imposed by society in the name of God. No more Moses, Christ or any higher law. We are both subject to and creator of a new order. We must learn to live alone, without the dream of God. Our only hope is to learn to manage the lottery, instead of blindly trusting it as if God were in control. We are machines, not created beings. Abandoning the pipe dream of a manager-God for tough, courageous action will lead us to authenticity. We must manage the lottery and no longer leave its selections to chance.

One wonders how Monod could use a word like authentic after such a stirring denial of the possibility of any spiritual or "higher" authenticity. Monod's human being is less than human, in the Christian sense. He says we are genetic machines, and we should define ourselves solely in terms of our genetic selection. Thus we must engineer that selection, for once it is made we are bound, doomed, to fulfill our own lottery drawing.

Monod waxes eloquent here. His conclusions are written in a tone that warns against dispute: the universe is a product of chance; it is time to wake up and join the game. But in urging these conclusions, Monod changes from scientist to philosopher. In the last chapters, Monod's discussion is a wonderful illustration of the phenomena of interpretation —of using the same data to come up with different conclusions. Christians believe, just as Monod, that life is "unique." There is no trouble at all with that . . . only with his impersonal lottery metaphor. Indeed, Monod's mathematical computation of the improbability of creation causes awe and amazement in a Christian reader. Creation was a unique and astounding, even mysterious event, just as Monod suggests.

What is disturbing, though, about Monod's book is the ease with which he moves from genetic specialist to prophet-at-large. In his conclusions, as his tone darkens and his voice becomes heavy with poetry, one feels him moving from the laboratory to the pulpit. His sermonizing quest for meaning is as fervent as the quest of those he despises as fools. And while his book is an exciting and helpful discussion of the new biological theories, all his metaphysical colorations are extra, added-on, not at all fresh-from-the-laboratory. He becomes too easily a social engineer, a pied piper, a priest, as he tells us what our new direction should be.

He pipes a mean tune. Like the best evangelist, he begins with warnings. We can no longer talk about meaning and purpose. We must discard the foolish notions of animism and theism, the foolish dreams of destiny and significance.

When we are reduced to appropriate distress, Monod offers himself. He has the knowledge and abilities, he assures us, to make some decisions that will help fill the void. For one thing, scientists can manipulate the lottery before the next drawing occurs, through genetic management of the human race. They can offer a "really 'scientific' social humanism" based upon genetic science alone. Science will build for us a new life over a crumbling foundation. Science will interfere with the lottery, helping humans to make educated genetic decisions before every new drawing.

> Where then shall we find the source of truth and the moral inspiration for a really *scientific* socialist humanism, if not in the sources of science itself, in the ethic upon which knowledge is founded, and which by free choice makes knowledge the supreme value—the measure and warrant for all other values?[13]

What do these words mean? Somehow science is the only certain thing left to us. Science can redirect our procreation and other crucial social habits. On the basis of scientific knowledge, Monod wants to set up a socialist system which will make all the genetic decisions about the future well-being of the race: who may live, whose genetic equipment must be sterilized, how to preserve the best of present cultures and civilizations through management of the game of chance. All we need do is exchange servitude to God for servitude to him. He, and his genetic engineers, will do the rest. In the laboratory they believe they can learn to manipulate the lottery to our advantage. This time, thanks to their efforts, nothing will be left to chance—or to God.

Why is his offer so unappealing? He says it is only because we haven't had time yet to forget the past. That will come with time. And since the "Kingdom Above" is gone for good —if it ever "was"—we must by ourselves "reconstruct the Darkness Below." We must make chance work in our favor. Science promises to engineer the game of chance, making a better world for all the products of the genetic lottery who call themselves human.

Monod's scheme is especially frightening because his choices of what ethics or morals should serve as a basis for future decisions will be imposed on us without our agreement. Science must ignore values as they have been traditionally received, says Monod. Proper management of the lottery is the only criterion for all decisions. So science creates its own values, as it goes along, basing every decision upon "adequate knowledge." The problem in the past was that we assumed a preordained moral code and fitted all knowledge into that code without being truly objective. Monod begins at the other end, starting with scientific knowledge, and ending with practical ethics, with no reference to higher "objectivity."[14] Science will tell us what to think and what to do. For there is no God, no truth, no meaning.

Monod asks too much. His system ignores personality, spiritual life, all intangible perceptions. Its sterility seems apparent. It is a one-sided view of personhood, and seems to ignore both personal responsibility and free choice (once our lottery drawing has occurred). Nevertheless genetic engineering of some sort is certain to become a reality and cannot be ignored.

Yet because Monod and others are determined to take things into their own hands, theists must stay with the discussion, learn the mechanics of DNA and become alert to the pursuit of new moralities through the new study of bioethics. Genetic management is certainly a crucial issue, and even promises to be beneficial. If the church drags its feet and fails to respond to the current issues posed by bioethics, the silence will be sad indeed. For Monod charges that the church has never been interested in joining hands with knowledge. Monod says there can never be a "proper wedding" of knowledge and value, so *value* must go—especially where the church has anything to say about it. Monod prefers that the church keep its distance on these issues. Value implies a God or higher law. Monod will only speak pragmatically.

Yet the proper balance of knowledge and value has been the painful quest of Christian scholars throughout the centuries. There are many who are still at work on it. Names that come quickly to mind range from the Renaissance ingenuity of Sir Thomas More's *Utopia* to recent writings from such scholars as C. S. Lewis and those Oxford Christians with whom he had frequent dialogue on these issues—Dorothy Sayers, J. R. R. Tolkien, Charles Williams, among them. G. K. Chesterton's masterful book *Orthodoxy* speaks convincingly to many of these contemporary questions as well. And other philosophers such as Austin Farrar and Jacques Maritain offer striking and cogent challenges to Monod's secular position. There are others. And there need to be more because the alternative is to give it all over to Monod and the secular engineers. Here is the challenge; value must be sustained as the church understands both the good and the dangers in genetic engineering.

What Monod really wants is a new kind of dictatorship, as full of difficulties as anything he wants to be freed from. The new dictatorship of scientific engineering ignores personhood. We are, indeed, "chemical machines," able to be manipulated before we are conceived or before we conceive again. Social engineering ignores too many things about humans—ignores "concrete experiences" (Whitehead would say), ignores spiritual inclinations, ignores the sense of personality. It is frightening when the social engineer asks to take on "priestly" functions, asks to be a substitute for all we have known, believed, experienced of the ways of the God of revelation.

Monod's stirring example suggests the degree to which one does all of science a grave disservice by assuming too easily that all a scientist's pronouncements must be embraced: the data may be solid; the pronouncements about that data may not be. Monod's awareness of the importance of genetics is of course a helpful and significant contribution. But the persuasive element in Monod's otherwise fascinating treatise is not of science. When one embraces the specialist (even the Nobel Prize winner) for his interpretation as well as his information, trouble awaits. No specialist should be trusted unquestioningly when he speculates about matters outside his area.

If we are not careful, we will allow ourselves to be ushered into a sterile technological world, stripped of human and spiritual qualities, and studded with the apparatus of the scientific explosion. The questions of value, purpose, meaning extend beyond the expertise of science.

Building No Boxes

The modern scientific outlook offers a variety of lessons. First, we know now that we can never know enough. We have come to appreciate the vastness of the world, of the universe, of our biological selves. We understand more than ever the difficulty of formulating laws that will stand still and work for us. We experience the surprise of new discoveries almost daily, discoveries that completely explode and alter some theory we thought was comfortably settled. We learn not to be surprised and perplexed. We see how hopelessly naive we have been; perhaps we are coming out of it. Just as the Ptolemaic astronomers once did, we have made God's world too simple, and we have once again done him a disservice by insisting that it had to be the way *we* described it. God has not slipped into ignominy. What has slipped are the artificial boundaries set up to contain him. Our miscalculations should not reflect badly on God but on us.

The "new" vastness of the universe in no way needs to alter our scriptural understanding of God. A first lesson it can teach us is not to measure Scripture by our faulty scientific understanding. We threw out a lot of perfectly good things in Scripture on the basis of some scientific principles which are now on shaky ground. Maybe we can reorder our priorities and refuse to measure the fantastic truths of Scripture by our very limited ability to understand the scientific underpinnings of God's universe. That was the purpose of God's revelation in Scripture—to give us a bridge across our ignorance and self-imposed sin to the very person of God. Neither he nor we had to wait until we "knew enough." Nor do we have to wait now, in our search to encounter God.

Second, science cannot forget about religion. Even Monod is compelled to grapple with it. The step from theoretical science to the religious question is a very short one. That shortness is seen by how quickly thoughtful scientists want to bridge the gap between the two.

Further, the very declaration that there are no metaphysical questions is itself a metaphysical statement. We are incurably metaphysical (incurably worshipful, Augustine said). The frustration of the scientific discipline is that it is not, by itself, able to make any metaphysical statements, except the very vaguest kind. Planck's "The Meaning and Limits of Exact Science" suggests exactly that. The scientist is frustrated in his yearning to move beyond his data.

The scientist who has struck a good balance has learned not to overvalue his limited findings, even though they are carefully tested and well substantiated. Planck is a paragon of such humility, just as his quantum theory is a milestone in physical theory. For even while knowing the significance of his achievement, this renowned scientist recognizes his limitations. In the end, science must look elsewhere to answer the final questions—unless it chooses to make science a new religion. If scientists sense the futility of that, they will have to continue looking beyond the laboratory for that elusive "something."

We are privileged to understand that in Scripture there is that more complete description of the nature of God and the meaning of life. But we need the lesson of humility just as much as anyone.

Lastly, let us recognize the considerable achievement of the scientific discipline and offer it our respect and attention. But let us see it for what it is—an important part, but still a part, of a much larger puzzle. It takes more than a formula of any size or shape or definition to hold all the secrets of the infinite God of heaven. We cannot quite get him to fit our small insights. He keeps bursting through them, time and again, dazzling us with infinitely more magnificent dimensions. The universe is not a vast whirling chaos; but we simply cannot imagine the kinds of equipment we would need to get it all together in our finite minds.

Still, we will always try. That is something of what it is to be human. That is why there will always be science. We are insatiably curious. We can never know enough. Every step beckons us to take one more. In our laboratories and libraries we will work all the time at measuring and mastering the vastness of the creation. That is good. Just so we never announce, one day, that we have got it all settled, that we have God in our box.

The Call of the Winds: Nature

3

Nature holds high sway among many thoughtful people today. Its magnetism reminds us again of the pied piper. Its proponents and devotees are legion, and its merits profound. Its charm is that it is the one thing we can count on in a world where everything else changes. For, unlike everything else, nature has always been there, waiting, calling us away from the hubbub of the noisy crowd. And at last some are beginning to hear. Some are beginning to come home.

Nature is beautiful and compelling. "I have been with you from the beginning," it seems to murmur, "and we belong *together*. The rest of this synthetic world is too unsteady to be counted on—but I have always been here." Its infinite cycles of life sustain our own lives. Should nature ever fail, we too would fail.

The return to nature is almost a religious one. The ecology crusades, the drive to sustain and preserve nature, to protect it—all these are linked to a religious quest. The love for the land, for the naturalness of earth-grown foods, for the joys of pastoral contemplation—all these rise from a new feeling of sacred respect. We are linked biologically and chronologically somehow with the great natural processes of life. And when all else seems to be crumbling, this can become a profound realization.

From the Ground You Were Taken

To the Christian that is just part of the story, though an immensely neglected part. It tells us that we are indeed closely linked to nature. "You [will] return to the ground," Scripture tells us, "for out of it you were taken; you are dust, and to dust you shall return." We are flesh, and "all flesh is grass.... The grass withers, the flower fades, when the breath of the LORD blows upon it; surely the people is grass," Scripture declares, reminding us of our natural sources (Gen. 3:19; Is. 40:6-7).

One has to agree that the rediscovery of our roots in nature is an important one. We had no clear idea, until the recent popularization of knowledge about the intricate balance of the life cycle, that our lives were so closely linked to all the creatures and chemicals of the earth. Or if we knew, we did not comprehend it. When algae can no longer survive in a distant ocean, the chain of life is weakened, and so are we. That we are formed of the dust of the earth means something very important. The Bible does not waste words. These statements are a significant piece of information about our origins.

What is more, when God was finished with all that he had made, he looked at all he had made and said that it was *very good*. All the works of his hands, together, as a whole, were very good. We belong to the created order. Our physical origins are in nature. We can, therefore, be enthusiastic about all the new clues pouring in regarding that link with nature, regarding nature's own infinite processes. For many, nature becomes an overwhelming and astounding study.

Yet how has nature been viewed? The eyes are generally sealed until a new awareness dawns. Many look at the ground and see only the surface they are walking on. They look at the earth and think of dirt, grime, black bugs. They look at the trees and see their shapes or even their shade—but they cannot describe the texture of the bark or remember if a woodpecker has left its holes anywhere on the trunk above. They throw away the burrs which catch in their scarves without thinking of spring or seeds, of the coming cycle of plants in the neighboring fields. Yet if no seeds returned to the earth we would surely die. Nature's details matter infinitely to survival—and we miss most of them.

Those who have learned to see again have their fingers on the very pulse of life. If they are floundering, confused, they feel relieved when they are with nature. They know themselves somehow in a new way. They know they are part of a process larger than themselves; they are part of the Process of Life Itself. For some, for a while, this is enough. Such knowledge becomes a religious experience, with the fruits of renewal and identity. Surrounded by change, impersonal technology, unparalleled inhumanity, nature is a stabilizer, a constant, a link with the heritage of the past and the future—a friend. Nature's friendship is impersonal, certainly. It does not exchange names. But it is a link to an ongoing and infinitely creative process, and it stands against chaos with the promise that "I belong to it," both in life and in death. Nature sustains, envelops, contains every living person.

That is wonderful. But it is not enough. The problems of personality, mind, conscience, destiny remain. Two things are true: we are dust; we are spirit. Christians know everything in nature from that perspective—know the world, and themselves from that double vision of their kinship with both earth and spirit, remember the Psalm which says, "My frame was not hidden from thee, when I was being made in secret, intricately wrought in the depths of the earth." The physical nature and the spiritual nature are both important to the purposes of God. It is true that one day the perishable nature will put on the imperishable, as 1 Corinthians tells us. In the message of redemption there is that hope of final transformation. But in the meantime, we are creatures of earth. The Bible declares us free to rejoice in the natural order, for God declared, "It is good."

Of course this is a different point of view from that of many popular naturalists. But as we begin to get close to their ideas, this Christian perspective will hold our thoughts in balance. We need to understand their deep appreciation for nature, and to share in their exhilaration as much as we can. And we will be freer to do this if we do not somehow feel we have compromised our Christian position by entering into their joy. We do not want to feel guilty when gripped by their excitement. Christians have the problem of reading too apprehensively and guiltily: sure we are somehow betraying our God if we enter too wholeheartedly into the pleasures of someone with a different perspective. We can avoid this uneasy feeling, this guilty suspicion of our motives, if we understand the biblical attitude toward nature. We can enjoy new discovery and still differ in interpreting that discovery. Ignoring the nature writers because they do not have a proper theological perspective is misguided. They still have a lot to say that is consistent with a biblical viewpoint.

For one thing, they remind us of our forgotten heritage. For another, they call us to re-estimate the value of our technology and the works of our own hands—to praise ourselves less. It is a humbling thing to realize that the works of our hands will perish and be forgotten by most, while nature will continue on. The nature writers despise a machine age in which we have allowed ourselves to become machines instead of warm throbbing mammals; we have abandoned our natural habitats of forests, fields and mountains for artificial ones of steel and concrete. No wonder we are unhappy!

These nature writers know how to meditate and think deeply. They can teach something of that art, the ability to contemplate, to look around and see the good that surrounds us. They know how to say "thank you" for these things even if they cannot name their Author. They are open to learning and seeing new mysteries day after day. That very openness is a worthwhile attitude. And the questions the nature writers always seem to come back to, always find unsettled, remind us—if not them—of that Author of nature. Their findings can serve to bring us round again to that very One we can never forget, the One we regard as Maker of all. That is our response to nature's one last unanswerable question. The naturalist's study can tell us much about *what* there is around us, about *how* nature operates—but nothing about *why*. The whole question of purpose is a blank. Nature is silent about "ends." We are turned back again to the resources of biblical revelation.

A Church to Walk In: Thoreau

Probably the nature writer closest to some inkling about the Author of all things is the "father of all modern nature writers," Henry David Thoreau. Writing one hundred years ago, he lived in a day when the people in his own town still knew their Maker's name. Yet he found these Christians cold and unappreciative of nature's secrets, too given to fatalistic gloom. He learned to shun their company. Of course, one might say, *they* cannot be blamed for his religious decisions; he could have remained among them if he chose, and tried to make a difference. His response to those Christians is a tremendous lesson for any who are tempted to shun Christians for their indifference and fatalism. What might the church be if people with special visions, such as Thoreau had, would determine to stay with her? These visionaries could correct much neglected imbalances in our view of things. As it is, we have to be corrected from the outside.

Thoreau's case is also a lesson in optimistic thanksgiving and appreciation of our natural heritage. He offers an alternative to the cramped and negative way of seeing life. "The mass of men," he reminds the Christians of his day, "lead lives of quiet desperation." And rather than argue with them about the validity of their Christian faith, he chose simply to strike off in an entirely different direction. His style was not the squabble or the verbal contest; his character, in this regard, was indeed admirable. We are sorry that he chose to withdraw, though. It was our loss.

He does mention the name of God from time to time. But

this is a God whose springs are in nature, who is part of and sometimes "equal to" nature. Thoreau mentions, too, a lot of the phrases from the old Christianity; but the phrases are poetic rather than theological. Nature supplies everything he could ever need. "It requires a direct dispensation from Heaven to become a walker," he says, paraphrasing a concept from the old New England faith. But nature is the *source* of his new life. "I think that I cannot preserve my health and spirits unless I spend four hours a day at least . . . sauntering through the woods, . . ." he proclaims in his finely written essay, "Walking." Nature has become his church. "I am alarmed when it happens I have walked a mile into the woods bodily without getting there in spirit," he laments. In nature he finds the truths of the spirit: "We saunter toward the Holy Land, till one day the sun shall shine more brightly than ever he has done, shall perchance shine into our own minds and hearts, and light up our whole lives with a great awakening light, as warm and serene and golden as on a bankside in autumn."

Yes, nature is a church for Henry Thoreau. It is far more than a physical reality. It is both physical and spiritual. He sees in it all those spiritual attributes which the local believers found at worship together on the Sabbath or in the private meditation of prayer. Thoreau was so close in time and location to historic Calvinistic Christianity that this carry-over of spiritual values into nature is quite understandable. Some have said that Thoreau and his circle evidenced a close kinship to Jonathan Edwards, that figurehead of Calvinism, because of Edwards's own very close feelings for nature. Spirit and physical nature are deeply intertwined in all of Thoreau's contemplation. This stance is a little different from the stress of our modern naturalists. They seem to concentrate more directly on the wonders of the physical world itself. For Thoreau nature was more a "medium" of unseen and spiritual realities. It was always impossible for him to separate the physical and the spiritual; they met in perfect correspondence.

The Gift of Ears; the Gift of Eyes

What, then, does nature "say"? Thoreau thought it "said" a lot. He thought it was fairly specific about some things. Modern naturalists are a little less sure about specific things. At least there is more variety of opinion on the subject. For them, nature raises more questions than it answers. Still, almost *all* nature lovers think nature is saying something. Thoreau was very confident of what he was hearing. "I believe that there is a subtle magnetism in Nature, which, if we unconsciously yield to it, will direct us aright. . . . There is a right way, . . ." he says in "Walking."[1] Nature tells him how to live the good life, how to live morally and ethically. Nature is not only its physical self, that chain of life which sustains us, but it also has a voice to speak to us. It is, or has, a spirit, as well as a physical reality. "I enter a swamp as a sacred place, a sanctum sanctorum," he says. "Nature is a personality so vast and universal that we have never seen one of her features." Nature provides a real spiritual backdrop, a personality whose magnetism attracts again and again.

If nature is not a "church" for the Christian, what then? What boon lies in these writings? While we arrive at truth differently than Thoreau does, preferring the specifics of biblical revelation, nature still has something for us. Thoreau does make a multitude of discoveries about the significance of nature. After all, he spent more than a year living alone in a cabin in the woods, thinking and writing continuously about what surrounded him.

He discovered the pleasure of building a cabin with his own hands, of rising early to hear the birds, of finding natural foods to sustain him. He learned to *listen*, to hear sounds we usually miss—bird voices, the whistling of telegraph wires, the intrusion of a far-off train whistle, the honking of the wild geese, the first note of the spring robin. He learned to *see*—pebbles, ants, the flight of a nighthawk, the "aching and sheaflike top of the woolgrass," the colorations of sand.

His memorable descriptions give us new eyes. If only we had seen that! If only *we* had noticed or heard:

> When the warmer days come, they who dwell near the river hear the ice crack at night with a startling whoop as loud as artillery, as if its icy fetters were rent from end to end, and within a few days see it rapidly going out. So the alligator comes out of the mud with quakings of the earth.[2]
>
> . . . I stood in the very abutment of a rainbow's arch, which filled the lower stratum of the atmosphere, tinging the grass and leaves around, and dazzling me as if I looked through colored crystal. It was a lake of rainbow light, in which, for a short while, I lived like a dolphin.[3]

This man with the gift of eyes is always turning what he sees into visions of imagination. He becomes a dolphin. He sees things turn into crystal or precious gems. He has both the gift of careful scientific observation and the gift of the dreamer. The two are a rare combination. For anyone even a little sensitive to nature, his words are a delight to read.

Like all nature writers who sing his tune, Thoreau recommends nature as a source of security and strength, a "port in a storm." When he sees the sunset, he wishes that every child could see it and be assured that it would "happen forever and ever." A town is "saved" by "the woods and swamps that surround it," he says. "I would have every man so much like a wild antelope, so much a part and parcel of nature, that his very person should thus sweetly advertise our senses of his presence, and remind us of those parts of nature which he most haunts." As we understand that we are "part and parcel of nature" we will find strength.

There is something to that. Not enough, surely. But some-

thing. We are, most of us, missing this whole side of our identity. Anyone, Christian as well as not, who begins to respond to the vision of Henry Thoreau recognizes that there is something excellent which we have missed. That recognition, so common to many readers of Thoreau, explains why after more than one hundred years his works are as modern and contemporary as they ever were. He is the pied piper of them all.

Lessons Learned in the Desert: Krutch

In his steps is a more contemporary piper for nature, the twentieth-century nature writer, Joseph Wood Krutch. Krutch takes up Thoreau's tune, and fits it to the city dweller, to most of us. We inhabit a world different from the world of Thoreau. There are fewer Walden Ponds to go to now. Suburbia has lapped them up. But we can at least have *window boxes*, urges Krutch!

There is no reason why we should also lose the art of the green thumb, even if we no longer live near a wood. Unless we reclaim a consciousness of nature, a sense of that closeness to the land which spurred our forefathers to spread across the plains, we may lose something forever that we cannot do without. If we relate only to machines and other human beings, and not with nature anymore, we will forget who we are; we will forget that nature is "the most significant background of human life." We will come to regard the works of our hands above the permanency of nature. We will forget that we are alive, and think only of ourselves as producers in a machine age. Technology is our biggest enemy. We have forgotten who we are. The essay, "In Back of Man a World of Nature" traces out the dangers which Krutch sees if we forget nature.

The cure for our forgetfulness and our machine-ness is in nature, just where Thoreau found it. Krutch especially recommends the desert. It has a mystique, he tells us, a way of speaking to us and giving us real "knowledge," mystical knowledge perhaps. It is not the knowledge of a textbook. It may even be something we cannot write down at all, but it is a special kind of truth about ourselves and about our world. "Only in nature do we have a being,"[4] he affirms in his book *The Voice of the Desert*. The truths of the desert, of conversation with nature, are not exactly religious truths. They don't even have the theological overtones of Thoreau's truths. They are more like truths of this world and do not necessarily suggest shining Universals or the "Transcendental Truth" with the same Thoreauvian confidence. Still, the desert truths can help us to live well amid physical realities.

Krutch calls some truths "metabiological truths." These are truths which point beyond us to some secret we do not understand. While we can no longer accept the notion of God, says Krutch, we can't exactly get along with materialism either. When we are in nature we feel that there must be more than that. There must be a larger secret. Surrounded by the desert and all it suggests of mystery, Krutch must still ask the higher questions. We have to "admit the mystical element" into our experience, he decides—after science seems to have forced us to rule it out. We are more than biology or chemistry.

Some secret exists behind nature, nature seems to say. A Christian reader may be reminded of Psalm 19: "The heavens are telling the glory of God. . . . Their voice goes out through all the earth." Or as the Living Bible paraphrases it, ". . . They are a marvelous display of his craftsmanship. Day and night they keep on telling about God. Without a sound or word, silent in the skies, their message reaches out to all the world."

But this message, this final truth, this something else beyond is very unspecific for Krutch. He seems more sure of what nature tells him for today than of what it says about its secret. The desert suggests the immediate values of courage and endurance. It brings us up against our limitations. It turns us in on ourselves and our own resources. And when we turn inward to reflect on values for today, we may even begin to find other enduring values besides the day-to-day ones. Krutch discovered in this way that he *had* to believe in the existence of a real, moral and ethical standard.

Something Behind

In another essay, "Life, Liberty, and the Pursuit of Welfare," he explains his conviction that justice is a real thing. He is sure that acts all have consequences, and that a person is responsible for his acts. The one who retreats to nature to contemplate will find that nature compels a person to speculate about the human race, the world and final values. Krutch illustrates the principle which Christians call "natural revelation." Such natural revelation does not begin to be specific enough, but it gives a person a good start.

Even with that start Krutch cannot help wondering about the bigger questions. The possibility of "ultimate meaning" tantalizes him. It will not leave us alone. While materialistic science has by now consigned all of creation to natural selection and has banished miracle and mysticism entirely, the lesson Krutch learns in the desert is that mere natural selection, mere materialism is not enough.

In an essay written within the last few years he declares that "there is far more reason to believe in than to reject" the existence of certain forces. He holds out for a belief in Purpose. He explains that this is not Purpose in the old Christian sense where God is outside the process. But he cannot accept either that Purpose is part of the natural world, inside it or inherent in it. That is not good enough. Instead he suggests a third possibility, that there is, somehow, "Something in the Universe" which causes man to be capable of Purpose and "effective intentions." It is a very reasonable supposition, he urges, that "something" should be "admitted" by the truth-seeker. That something is at least the "advantage bestowed by purposefulness," he calls it. He means that at the very least we have to admit that people believe in Purpose, act purposefully, that there does seem to be a Purpose, that it is just blind stubbornness to refuse the obvious.

Krutch remembers the words of others who came to the same conclusion. He is impressed by the words of anthropologist and naturalist Loren Eiseley who also came at last to suspect the existence of a "Great Face Behind." It is clear, Krutch concludes, that "not *all* scientists believe the last word has been said on the question."[5] There may indeed *be* "Something Behind."

Now that is very good news. Because if some scientists and modern nature lovers cannot rest without some such idea, then there is still room for conversation—conversation in which the Christian may be more welcome than he thought if he can tread carefully and handle the issues intelligently. Both Krutch, Loren Eiseley and others like them seem to wish, whenever they come right up to it, that they could be theists. They have seen too much at work in the living fabric of nature to be able to shuffle it all off as accident or chance or pure mechanics. They really want to find a basis for values, a basis for emotions, a basis for the amazing force of personality, for those intense desires which continually lure them ahead to what they cannot quite grasp.

Amazed at the Dream Animal: Eiseley

Loren Eiseley's book, *The Immense Journey*, is a very moving account of that quest for the meaning and sources of life. He recalls standing one day above a large geological slit in the earth, looking down to see an ancient skull staring up at him. That moment, that encounter, between the living and no-longer-alive spoke to him of an unbroken bond of life between them; he thought of the endless questions of the past and of the future, along the journey of earthly life. His book follows the course of that life from very early ages to the dramatic coming of the human race. He traces out some of the mysteries as well as the discoveries which he made as he investigated that immense journey. His account is beautiful and impressively written.

Some of his readers will be troubled. Eiseley accepts, after close study of the origins of the human race, a modified version of the theory of Alfred Russel Wallace. Wallace, an evolutionist, a believer in natural selection and one of Darwin's contemporaries, held out for an idea which would still allow human beings to have divine origin. Darwin had ardently opposed him on this. But now, in this much later time, Wallace's theory seems better to Eiseley.

Wallace argued that we mortals had a recent and sudden development, and that the sudden explosion of our capacious brain size was a unique and remarkable happening. Darwin had held out for a much earlier and small-brained human race that evolved far more gradually. Although Darwin's theory is what many of us heard in school, recent archaeological investigation has failed to substantiate it, says Eiseley.

Instead it looks to him as though the very earliest human beings had a remarkable brain size, a capacity even larger than what was needed in a primitive society. Today, with our capacity to design computers and split atoms, we have essentially the same brain as the earliest known humans. We are as we have always been, declares Eiseley. Of course, Eiseley is no "divine originist" as Wallace was, but he finds Wallace's theory remarkably accurate. The coming of "the dream animal," as Eiseley calls him, seems to be a unique and amazing historical event.

This "dream animal" seems to have left almost no clues to its origin, Eiseley observes. There are lots of monkey skulls but almost no human fragments to help solve the puzzle. In fact, the arrival of mankind at all on the scene is a most unusual, and probably unrepeatable, biological event. (This is the same observation Monod makes.) For the human race as we know it to have emerged at all, to have survived at all, required not one but four conditions: (1) the brain had to treble in size (from a prehuman skull); (2) this had to happen *after* birth, or mother and infant would both have died; (3) a longer period of initial growth (childhood) had to become a social habit; and (4) family bonds had to become permanent rather than seasonal if the helpless infant was to grow to adulthood. It is simply amazing to Eiseley that all four of those conditions converged. If *any* of them had not occurred, humanity would never have emerged.

It is such "coincidences" as these that make people like Eiseley and Krutch believe in Purpose rather than in blind chance. Humanity's very appearance signals a movement of Purpose, a change upward rather than downward. Surely it can't be for nothing that it happened. Eiseley is impressed with the principle of organization, that mysterious principle he says leaves all other mysteries of life stale and insignificant by comparison. He suspects that Organization is something more than mere natural selection, even that it might have been "there" before the beginning, whatever that was, of life. He is impressed too with the persistence of Pattern throughout all the ages.

Still he cannot feel sympathy with the persistent attempts of theologians to focus the story of creation around a human-centered universe, to say that all of the discoveries of prehuman ages somehow prefigure humanity. He sees that version as an irresponsible attempt to manipulate the facts. So, he dismisses the idea of divine origin as an impossible wish.

Eiseley's dismissal of divine origin seems somehow unsatisfactory. There are many unsolved questions lying between his anthropological version and the theistic version. Many loose ends still demand, or at least allow, a divine hypothesis—loose ends which Eiseley himself admits.

He finds order, pattern and purpose almost undeniable. Indeed, most of this book is a piece of speculative amazement at the phenomena of creation. Eiseley is drawn by an irresistible "something" on every hand. He decides the whole process, humanity included, is a *unique* and *unrepeatable* event.

This is no problem for someone who holds that God did it. It makes more sense that way. Christians prefer it to be unique. That conclusion may trouble the deist or the Unitarian who sees the universe in the old way, as a perfectly predictable giant clock. But the biblical way can get on without the clock, the mechanism anybody could understand. The book of Job, for instance, suggests that we are presumptuous to think we understand the secrets of the Almighty too easily. Job declares in repentance, "I have uttered what I did not understand." Christians are glad to recognize that creation is mysterious, unrepeatably unique, even beyond our complete understanding. We can live with that.

The lesson here is that the puzzle pieces are still fragmentary. For Christians or naturalists to rush too hastily to their own special conclusions would be unthinking. It is God's world. Our confidence in him should waylay our temporary feelings of insecurity. What both views need is a good dose of suspended judgment.

A Seed Pod, a Grasshopper Leg—and Wonder

In the meantime, there is real beauty in our encounter with nature. Eiseley's book itself, once we have gotten over the hurdles of interpretation, is a beautiful rehearsal of the way a sensitive human being responds to his natural surroundings. His account is deeply moving.

When he comes upon birds, he is moved to awe and hushed emotion. The pigeons flying into the early morning sky of New York City astound him. A crow which meets him suddenly at eye level in a dense fog emits a wondrous cry of disbelief, suspecting this man must be flying too! When a raven savagely devours a nestling before a horrified band of winged mourners, a song sparrow breaks into a piercingly beautiful song of sorrow. Eiseley is amazed at the emotional sensitivity of these creatures.

In the most moving account of all, he releases a captured hawk into the sky and as he hears its mate cry out, he knows that a faithful bird has circled above for hours, waiting. He is stunned. We are stunned. It is a great mystery. What can it mean?

That question, "What can it mean?" becomes a haunting one for every person who is alive to nature. As Eiseley puts on his coat and journeys across a wall into the woods on a Saturday, he holds a seed pod and a grasshopper leg, and wonders. He is sure now, he says, that life is "not as natural as it looks." There is much more.

We aren't anywhere near getting the secret down in a neat formula, after all. Anyone who walks out in nature guesses that. Science, muses Eiseley, has dismissed miracles as mythology, but science has created a mythology of its own. The materialist view is no better than the old theory, he suspects—maybe even worse. They are wrong, says Eiseley, who assume there is no mystery. There is a very great mystery. It is this mystery, he says, that keeps him wandering in pastures and weed-thickets instead of through the more fashionable mazes of the laboratory. He has ceased to believe that the final secret is in the chemical brew of test tubes. Somewhere among the abandoned beetle shells and grasshopper legs, he muses, is something that is not accounted for very clearly in that modern laboratory. Even after the final, minute, dissection, "the cloud will still veil the secret." And only along the edges of a field, as you walk in nature, after the frost, will you find little "whispers of it."[6]

There are many new laboratory discoveries, several every day, but what the "inexperienced reader may not comprehend," he warns, is that none of them is *the* secret. Instead, the growing list of secrets or discoveries only emphasizes the enormous complexity of *the* secret. Even if, sometime, the slime of the laboratory suddenly crawls under our direction, even if we claim someday to have "made life," the secret of that life will still have eluded us. Eiseley hopes we will then have the sense to recognize we haven't got it even yet. The materialist must learn to wonder how in the world the thing he calls "dead"matter was able to raise up song sparrows and fiddling crickets and wondering humans. The materialist too must learn at last that perhaps there is still some "Great Face Behind."[7]

The secret of nature and of life is enormous. We are not anywhere near it, with all the laboratory equipment in the world. The devoted follower of nature must at last stop in amazement—and simply wonder. Eiseley's *Immense Journey*, along the remotest pathways of nature, is a testament to that wonder and to that last unanswered question.

The speculations of Eiseley and others increase the certainty that nature speaks powerfully. Nature speaks of secrets, of mysteries, of something greater than ourselves. God exhorted Job to awe at those secrets in the famous Old Testament speeches: "Is it by your wisdom that the hawk soars, and spreads his wings toward the south? Is it at your command that the eagle mounts up and makes his nest on high?" (Job 39:26-27). Job and we ought to understand that here are wonders and spectacles beyond our grasp or our control. Like Job, we learn humility, for "his ways are past finding out."

The Mute Gospel

The key to our confrontation with nature, though, may lie in that very word Thoreau uses to describe its charm. "A farm is a mute gospel," he says. Nature's gospel is *mute*. It keeps the secret. It does not give it out. It is that silence, that last unspoken mystery, that confounds. All who come to nature are confounded by its silence on the final question. Here is a gospel, but without content, without specifics. Nature only asks the question. It refuses to divulge the answer. We find no help without some supernatural revelation to interpret. Alone in nature, one stops at last before the door of the mystery.

The limits of nature are seen in several areas. First, nature provides a significant background for all activity. It gives us a certain new sense of identity. There is no denying that. But while nature can tell us we are animals and not machines, it cannot tell us what a human being is. It does not give much clue to the meaning of personality, or lend much support to the quest for personal significance, above and beyond the physical. It suggests that there is another dimension, but it cannot help us find it.

Second, nature is also unable to soothe our apprehension in the face of death. It is not comforting enough to say we are part of the life cycle or that everything dies. Nature seems an enemy, not a friend, in the giving of death. That the life cycle goes on without me does not answer the personal need for a unique and individual significance.

The third limitation is that nature is not always a friend, even in life. Sometimes it deals the very blow that spells a catastrophic loss of all that I love most, in a storm, a fire, a cancer. It seems at times to strike without regard for persons at all. If nature is the sole source of religious affirmation and confidence, I cannot feel very secure or comforted.

Finally, nature does not tell me how to act. Well perhaps vaguely, if Krutch is right about nature telling him that acts have consequences. Paul says in Romans that the most untutored person has enough light to know right from wrong. Krutch says that nature tells him many general things about behavior, and about people: that we all believe there is a difference between justice and injustice, that there is something higher than the purely material in this life. C. S. Lewis believes too that almost everyone knows how to say, "That's not fair!" no matter what his cultural background is. He agrees with Krutch that everyone knows a lot of things about right and wrong almost naturally.

Still, there is something missing. Beyond the idea of right and wrong is the need for some specifics. Nature does not provide those specifics. For this reason a revelation, such as the Old Testament code of the Ten Commandments or the words of Jesus Christ in the New Testament, supplements nature and makes its twinges of conscience *specific*: Thou shalt do no murder. Revelation gives a specific, sensible, and universal code that can fit any culture. Nature needs revelation.

Nature without revelation leads to a kind of relativism and subjectivism in which everybody is a law unto himself. Each one takes the generalities of nature and works them out differently. This is one of the notable characteristics of the nature writers—an intense subjectivism and individuality. Now subjectivism, experiencing one's convictions, can be good. But there needs to be some agreement on the larger issues; there needs to be some balance between individualism and community. Nature, by itself, is unable to provide this balance.

What is still lacking is that theological explanation of the creation, fall and redemption of the world, the assurance that God holds out both a universal and a personal salvation. In that affirmation lies the value of individual human beings. There lies the comfort of a God who cares. There lie the specific morals that nature only hints at. Yet for the good nature does, we will henceforth "think on these things." We understand anew that we will not know ourselves unless, both literally and mentally, we put ourselves back into the context of nature. The nature writers assist us to that insight.

A World Come of Age: Humanism

Meaning of the Twentieth Century, feels that the sudden shift in civilization points without question to such a new day. The twentieth century is in the middle of a great transition, a human transition as enormous as the first great transition from precivilized to civilized society which began five or ten thousand years ago. That first great transition is almost complete in our century, except for isolated pockets. But these pockets contain a small five per cent of the world population. The rest of the world, says Boulding, may be termed "civilized." We have moved first from a primitive and Neolithic lifestyle to a civilized, agricultural one, and at last have become an urban and highly technical people. We have made astounding leaps in our short history.

The proof of this second major transition, he explains, is all around us. Agriculture is no longer the predominant way of life. It is only a support-activity for other things. Primarily it supports the knowledge industry. We now have time for such a thing because the margin of life is no longer precarious. We have time for bigger, more long-range dreams and plans. We are ready to develop.

In fact, Boulding continues, today we are far along in this second great transition. There is no choice about it. We have passed the crossroads. The date of crossing is probably within living memory of most readers of his book, says Boulding. We have lived through a dramatic moment. At last, he declares, it will be possible for us to begin developing our full potentials and capacities—no longer having to direct our full attention to the demeaning business of survival. Poverty, disease, famine, possibly even war, he says, can be negotiated or solved. Skylab experimenters hope very shortly to predict and control famine through their observations, for instance.

Now if the question is one of controlling and using technology for the benefit of more and more people, Boulding's point is hard to dispute. It is already true that many people

4

There is talk now about a new humanism, about "man c
of age," about a new "kingdom of man on earth." It is bl
stirring talk and it calls forth all the hopes that ever rose w
in us. We would like so much for things to turn out all ri
We really want to be optimists.

But this optimism is an entirely new kind. It is an c
mism that things will turn out all right even without God
fact maybe even better than with him. It is an entirely ea
centered, life-centered optimism. It is simply the belief
as the race "matures," on the other side of the Knowle
Explosion, we will "come into our own."

The new optimism has to forget a lot of things to say th
things like Auschwitz and Hiroshima and the Berlin \
and all the little incidents in our own day that make a
optimists tremble and wonder if they have dreamed t
lives away in vain. But the new optimists have a way of
getting those things. Their vision of the New Human u
them on and on.

They believe history is on their side. They forget Au
witz and Hiroshima and look at other signs of the times.
bigger sweep of destiny outweighs the isolated horrors,
say. We have come to the place in our evolution where
are ready to use our mental powers for a great consum
tion. At last, after the Knowledge Explosion, our tools
almost sharp enough to set things straight.

The Second Great Transition: Boulding

World change proclaims the coming of this new day,
some of the historians. Economist Kenneth Boulding, in

spend less and less time grinding out a bare existence. And with more time the prophets fondly hope that we may at last discover *what it is to be human.* Perhaps, they hope, we may become so much more than we already are that the term *genius* will be meaningless as a mark of the unusual.

Of course, "being human" is not an easy thing. The new humanists recognize that. Boulding is not naive about the obstacles in the path. He recognizes that war, overpopulation, and even technology itself may eventually stand in the way of such marvelous development of human potential. But he does not believe that such threats ought to prevent one from making a mighty effort in that direction. The race is ready, and we have the time. We *must* make a new beginning. There seems to be no way back. The coming of the Knowledge Explosion is irreversible.

Building a New Religion: Huxley

Our recognition of this explosion is probably long overdue. Boulding's comments are a kind of echo to an earlier twentieth-century prophet whom many avoided as an evolutionist and so failed to hear. Julian Huxley had already announced this new day. Basing his prophecy on his own biological studies, Huxley was talking of a new humanism three decades ago. Foreshadowing Boulding, he too viewed humanity at the very brink of a dramatic historical moment. In *Religion without Revelation*, especially in the two essays "Developed Religion" and "Evolutionary Humanism," he explains his prediction.

A new movement which he calls "transhumanism" is upon us. The term he chooses suggests the magnitude of the change he is proclaiming. The present day, he declares, is the last period in the long history of the evolution of the human race. We have at last taken a step toward self-consciousness. We face the prospect at last of becoming fully mature, of becoming *managing-director of the whole cosmic process*. At last we are ready, through the increase in knowledge available in this century, to open ourselves to the vast possibilities of consciousness and personality. The most fortunate people alive today are still living far below their capacities; it is time to fulfill those latent talents and endowments. We must transcend ourselves and realize the new possibilities "of" and "for" our human nature.[1]

Stirring predictions! We would all like to be more fully human. But it sounds almost too utopian. Still, when Boulding's more objective historical documentation joins forces with the biological speculations of Julian Huxley, the prospect is hard to resist. Perhaps the historical moment does suggest the possibility of change.

The troubling thing about Huxley's comments, though, is the confidence they display in the scientific process to implement these changes. Huxley is the type of social engineer recommended by Monod in *Chance and Necessity*. Huxley's new humanism is based almost entirely upon science, and any spiritual qualities are the result of "scientifically conducted observations" about the kind of spiritual values more useful to the New Human. Since all religions are the product of our creative minds, says Huxley, it will be up to science to provide the data, derived from personal and collective experience, to assist in "building a new religion." Science will contribute its hard-won, well-tested knowledge and its own "disinterested devotion to truth" in the services of a new, earth-centered "religion of mankind."

Developed religion must not be content to leave its religious life "chaotic and unordered" with "loose ends unconnected with the rest of reality," Huxley warns. He thinks the historical church has always refused to be interested in knowledge and has always disliked talking about new things. Further, developed people should be concerned with general ideas of truth, beauty, goodness, holiness, unity, and then too with the conquest of nature, the development of the mind and the well-being of socially united individuals. Religion's goal should be the "flowering of the individual." It should help us build a personality. Then we must also reach beyond ourselves to create and preserve beauty, conserve natural resources, care about things beyond our own private lives. Thus, Huxley concludes, we are two things: we are individuals but we are part of a larger whole. We need a careful balance between the two. And if we get close to this balance, we may be getting close to something Huxley calls "destiny" or the "final religious question."[2]

Huxley thinks these are goals the historical church often chose to forget about. Now it is true, the church is properly concerned first of all with an other-worldly-relationship. That is the heart of Christian theology. But at the same time, the fruits of Huxley's religion ought also to be the fruits of Christian religion. If they are not, we do indeed have an undeveloped religion. Perhaps Huxley has noticed something important. Maybe our disregard for those things has led him to believe Christianity has passed its prime.

The most important difference between the Christian Human and this New Human, however, must be pointed out. The Christian idea of personal development has always been squarely based on the concept of God as the Author of the created order, as the center of all knowledge, as the giver of eternal life now and beyond that created order. By contrast, the new humanism places the New Human Race at the center: humans are the focus and end of the new quest. If we worship at all, we worship the creation, not the Creator. We enjoy the emotions of awe, mystery, dread and wonder—at ourselves—for our part in the ongoing cosmic process. And when our part is over, that is the end. No eternal expectations at all.

Even so, the new humanists refuse to brood over the darker view (even if it is there) because their faith is in science and the present and the prospect of the future. If there is no God to supply eternal certainty, experiment and observation can instead provide at least a limited certainty. What we build might just endure. In that hope the new humanists build and plan.

Consciousness III Lives: Reich

The works of these new utopians are nothing like the darker utopian works which came before them—books like Orwell's *1984* and Aldous Huxley's *Brave New World*. No one reading these books could have missed the bitter warnings. They foretold only wide-scale threats to personal freedom and dignity. Big Brother loomed ominously in the background. The dehumanized laboratory people of *Brave New World* were grossly distasteful. We knew we should reject them.

But these newer humanists are more hopeful—and terribly serious. They really hope to prevail. And they think that will be a good thing. They don't believe *their* way will be dehumanizing. They think their method can correct mistakes and make better people. We have the technical equipment, and the time, to make it all come true, they say. *If we dare.*

And some do plan to dare! The sudden and sweeping rise and fall of Charles A. Reich's *The Greening of America* is some measure of the new mood. It is not a book of despair. It is a book for visionaries. Youth by the thousands read it recently, talked about it and seemed to find new hope. And while the discussion has died down, its convictions remain. While many other readers have wanted to dismiss the book as a freakish manifestation of the drug culture, it is more serious than that. It is a kind of indicator of the new direction.

The book explains that there are three basic attitudes in America, all existing side by side: Consciousness I, II and III. Consciousness I was probably authentic in its beginning, says Reich. It represented the frontier experience, rugged individualism, early religious values which were deeply felt and lived. But alas, Consciousness II invaded, and life became more technological, "citified," corporate, politically complex. After World War 2, and an increasing takeover by huge corporate interests of more and more corners of private life, the small town farmer or small merchant became a vanishing species. Consciousness II prevailed.

But Consciousness II squeezed people to death. They lost their sense of pride in work and became absorbed by the assembly line, the company, or the soil-bank program. One could no longer say, "This I have done," and point with pride to some piece of his own work. People became lost souls. The old goals of Consciousness I just were not workable anymore.

Now there is hope, says Reich. Consciousness III is coming into its own. People are realizing their alienation and seeking to rediscover their authentic personalities. They are reaching out beyond Consciousness II for new awareness of life—of people, of the human experience, of joy in the land, of creative work. They are finding themselves through experiences of adventure and travel, life in harmony with nature, physical activity, new modes of dress, a flowering of sexual activity, identification with the changing seasons, rhythm, dance, ceremony, ritual, music, awe, wonder and reverence. Most of all, they are believing again in the possibility of being human.

Now Reich may be a poor social analyst or too simplistic, as some say. But he does a good job of summing up the new dream. People may be tired of his book—but not of the dream. "Finding the true self" still makes articles in the popular magazines and still brings people out for adult classes in search of new creative experiences. And if we can continue to stay warm, fed, alive and out of war, the trend is likely to continue.

There is plenty here for Christians. A little more awareness of the cycle of the seasons, a little more feeling for rhythm and music, a little more respect for the created order, a heightened spirit of adventure—who doesn't welcome such stirring innovations in a drab and humdrum life? On the other hand, there is a problem too. The new humanism handles moral and ethical questions differently than Christianity does: we are responsible only to ourselves for our actions, not to God or to God's revealed criteria for those actions.

Still, many of the things the new consciousness asks for are quite in line with the Christian respect for creation, and for its Author. Did not Christ himself say that he came to set people free? Self-actualization, maybe? Did not David learn to magnify God for the works of creation, and even dance and sing and shout before the Lord, learning to worship with mind and body together? Did not the most skillful artisans of the land bring their handwork for building the temple? The Scriptures speak of whole people, joined body and mind in the experience of life with God. If God made us in his image, as the Scriptures say, what are the qualities inherent in that image which we still do not know, until we become more fully human? Christians have to say that God favors creativity, whether in art or music or in the human personality. He is Lord of all.

We belong to the new consciousness, and we do not belong. First, we cannot violate God's moral commands. Second, we know that we are more than chance biological happenings. We know our origin. We understand that we are God-created personalities. So we, too, rejoice in creation.

Blueprint for a New Society: Skinner

Expressing the desire for a new humanism from a very different angle is Harvard psychologist B. F. Skinner. He first wrote a book giving a formula for New People in the 1940s, though nobody listened very well. There wasn't much interest in a serious utopia then. We had been through too much.

But now, thirty years later, he is coming into his own. And a more recent book fleshes out the formula of his first. In fact, Skinner's works sound a warning to us. His New Human is a mechanical person stripped of what he calls "freedom and dignity," yet fulfilling many of the criteria of the new consciousness.

The brave new books are *Walden II* and *Beyond Freedom and Dignity*. *Walden II* was written and first published in 1948, but was eclipsed by the popularity of *1984* and *Brave New World*. People preferred the darker utopias then, in the gloomy years after the worldwide holocaust they had hoped in vain would be the last war. *Walden II* sounded too self-assured, too hopeful. It took itself too seriously. People were building bomb shelters and learning to listen for communists and mafia contacts in their own neighborhood. The prevailing pessimism left little appetite for utopian prattle.

Now we have returned, at least for a while, to a taste for fantasy, or for fantasy made practical. *Walden II* presents a method for making the dream of self-actualization come true. And since this is its goal, there is something far more serious hiding behind the fantasy. Skinner pushes the new secular humanism to a disturbing conclusion.

His blueprint for a new society achieves the goals of Consciousness III through strict behavioral engineering. Yet it is curious that his carefully engineered society holds the contemporary imagination at the same time that the individualism of the new consciousness does. How can this be? Perhaps the reason lies in ends rather than in means. Skinner's new society, typified in Walden II, exemplifies many of the same fruits as does Consciousness III. Yet while Consciousness III finds personhood through creative release from restraint, Walden II engineers these fruits through careful human control. Reading his book, many have been impressed with the quality of life Skinner proposes. They admire it not for the way the quality is achieved, but for the sanity of its ends. Let us try it, anything, to better the human condition, they agree.

Incredible, we may say. How can one assure happiness through human management? But actually it is not so far-fetched at all. We live in a time when the social engineers want to be at work. Their experimental science is already in progress. They fully believe that we can be conditioned to like whatever they decide is best for us. The proposals are still on the drawing boards. But the future portends government-directed euthanasia, abortion, sterilization (of persons with defective "genes"), all to make us more "compatible" with our environment.

Genetic engineering is dreaming of these things—even of altering the structure of the brain! These may be coming our way as actualities. The trouble is, these decisions hinge profoundly on moral and ethical values. And the new behaviorist is going to make decisions according to what is "scientifically best" for mankind—not according to moral and ethical values. We could be coming into an entirely new moral climate—and moving toward it quickly.

Walden II, to be sure, is "only a novel." That is a relief. But it represents more. The main character, Burris—a parody of the author's first name—visits a utopian community managed by his old friend Frazier—a parody of Skinner's middle name. Frazier is a bumbling, embarrassed, almost incompetent leader with an unremarkable personality. But the community runs well in spite of him. So Burris is unimpressed at first, because Frazier is such a dud.

But he observes how the community is run. Beginning as infants, babies are raised together in communal nurseries, according to strict standards. They gradually join small groups of children who play and learn together and at last become "whole" adults who marry together and bear children, who begin the cycle all over again. Every person is viewed as an unfolding personality, and the community helps him unfold and become himself. Each member does a lot of different things—from manual labor to playing the clarinet, to painting, to gardening. There is no neurosis here and no competition. Everyone is becoming himself, not trying to be better than someone else.

At last Frazier explains that the community really works because it is based on a "perfect idea." Frazier can never be perfect because he was not raised in this community. To be an ideal person one has to be born there. Otherwise he will be defective, like all other human beings. Burris looks very hard at the idea. Out in the world where he came from there is no way to get rid of personal defects. Here, he can at least make a new beginning. He can try to become himself. So Burris becomes a convert to the new human engineering.

In many ways we have to applaud this notion of becoming yourself rather than beating your brains out trying to beat someone. It makes a lot of good sense. A lot of the other ideas make good sense too. There is a real concern with diet and nutrition. There is preventive medicine and dental hygiene. There is encouragement and discipline—in good balance. There is a sense of community and a sense of personality—in good balance.

Who Engineers the Engineers?

Yet there is something ominous about all this. This entire community is built upon what Skinner calls a "powerful science of behavior." Skinner believes that the whole human personality can be designed and engineered from the outside, by an intricate system of social pressures. We cannot handle atomic research, ecological crisis or capitalistic greed because our personalities are deficient—we have not developed as fast as our technology has. So our target ought to be ourselves. We have to catch up with our inventions. If we don't, all we can hope for is greed, corruption, breakdown, jealousy, war—on a personal and an international scale. We need help.

But what kind of help? The experts can help us out by using social engineering to manipulate and change our behavior. But which experts? Who are they? What are their motives? What permanent and irreversible changes will they make? And what ethical and moral values will be used to make these choices? We fear the social engineer. Skinner tries to be reassuring. Those with the tremendous responsibility of social engineering, he feels sure, will quickly learn how much better unselfishness works. It is a matter of experimental fact: unselfishness works better! No need to fear. So we'll just have to believe, says Skinner, that the social engineers can be trusted; and we will just have to trust them to choose for us.

We wish we could. Skinner pleads his case well. But there is that little slip twixt the cup and the lip that holds us back. There is danger here. For Skinner's social engineer has a completely different idea about what people are. We are machines. We do not have a divine origin. Our nature is caused entirely by our environment. If one wants to change what we are, one simply changes our environment. There is no definition for *human*. We are what we make ourselves—no, not even that—we are what our *environment* makes of us. We are pawns.

That is all there is to it, says Skinner. Ask all the other questions you like, social engineering is the real thing. What about life? death? meaning? Never mind. This is what we know. It will have to do. If we want to call ourselves "children of God," we will just have to get over it.

Somehow this is unsatisfactory. We know in our hearts we are more than machines. We are convinced of it, no matter what the laboratory says. These human engineers trust too exclusively in what the laboratory tells them. They believe too easily in what they "see" in the laboratory; they trust *their* interpretations too easily. They have not understood their limitations as scientists, limitations the researchers in advanced physics have understood for years. The problems of accurate observation, in fact the whole process of testing and measuring, is on questionable ground. The laboratory method of human engineering is in trouble, unless it learns its tentativeness. For the laboratory experiment may yield much useful information, but it cannot be trusted for everything.

The most serious gap in the laboratory-engineered New Human is the loss of the divine dimension, that sense of awe, mystery and divine communion which has fired people through the ages. Skinner dismisses all that. In his community there is no religion. Instead, there is community ritual. The center of the ritual is group loyalty not divine loyalty. Family culture is the replacement for religion. Its goal is ethical training and not wisdom or a sense of the sacred. At least Julian Huxley thought we needed a sense of the sacred. Even that is gone now. If anyone comes to Walden II hankering after religion, he is tolerated until he can give it up, just as he soon gives up smoking and alcohol. A person in Walden II just won't need God anymore.

What is the meaning of life then? Don't ask, Skinner advises. In fact he refuses to answer. But that is no answer at all. That Skinner refuses to discuss the theory behind his idea suggests a serious flaw somewhere. There are some really large questions here: Why do humans function best this way? What is the purpose of the community? What are the highest goals in life? Skinner answers: *any goals will do*—just so they work! He is all practice and no theory. He gives no basis for human existence.

Ethics Reduced to Survival

His newest book, *Beyond Freedom and Dignity*, illustrates the fundamental difficulty of human engineering. It pushes all the difficulties of the behavioral position to the extreme.

It clearly traces the dead end to which it may be leading. Whenever the question, "Why?" comes up, Skinner replies, "Never mind why." We do not need such an explanation to function.

Beyond Freedom and Dignity is an overwhelming book. Skinner tells us pointblank that we are machines, ready and waiting for manipulation and engineering. The point is to give us "good engineering" before the bad takes over. If we know we are merely pawns of environmental pressure, we will soon learn to stop using foolish words like *freedom* and *dignity*. We are not free and never were. We become what our environment forces us to become. So if we give up the illusion of free choice, we will be in a healthier frame of mind. (All those so-called "free choices" are just things that happen when a series of pressures or "contingencies" come together and drive us to make certain choices.) By overcoming this illusion of freedom, we can learn to "direct the contingencies" and make our "machines" work better than if left to the willy-nilly forces playing upon us. Environment will always press in, so why not make that pressure the "best pressure possible." Science can help us to determine what those "best pressures" should be.

Once we understand "scientifically" what goes into the making of choices (though not free choices, mind you), we can get hold of the process of building humans, we can manage and govern all choices (ours and everyone else's) and "make" things happen the way the experts think they should.

The experts? There is the whole question of values again. What is a good choice? On what basis will we choose the good and strive for it? Skinner's only answer is that whatever works for survival is good. Whatever decreases the chances of survival is bad. That is a rather thin foundation for moral decisions. All discussion of good or of evil melts now into that one word: *survival*.

This kind of technologically based new humanism takes away personal freedom. But Skinner sees this loss of freedom as a good thing. Under the illusion of freedom we gave ourselves too much credit. We praised ourselves when we did whatever we did. We are neither responsible nor deserving of praise, urges Skinner. When we finally learn the lesson of behavioral science, we will see there is no credit and no blame. Human responsibility does not exist. No more need to worry about it, he urges. Our chief problem is not being responsible but making the best possible use of our "machine"—by putting ourselves at the disposal of the experts and learning new patterns of behavior.

There is no need for either guilt or false pride. Our choices are very predictable outcomes of the contingencies. If we are not happy with the outcome, we can allow the human engineers to change the structure of those contingencies. We can get busy with the real business of life—submitting ourselves to the personality design which is best for us and for the people who have to live with us. We will then make the right choices. (Never mind the definition of *right*; right is whatever seems to work best.)

Now at last maybe we will see truly humble people, Skinner hopes: people who understand the principles of human design will no longer insist on having fame all the time; nor will they care if we fail to notice them. That would be a wonderful surprise.

The Dimensions of Divine Creaturehood

Yes, in a sense we have to agree. The loss of dignity—of a certain kind—could be a very good thing. We would be able to tolerate people much better. But it depends upon what one means by *dignity*. Skinner uses the word mainly to mean "pride." But Christians also use the word *dignity* to explain our origin, to explain that people are made in the image of God. That is a different concept from pride. If we remembered we were made in the image of God, perhaps we wouldn't brag about ourselves so much either—as if the world were made for us only. No, we did not make the world. God did. We are not finally responsible for how things turn out. God is. But we have dignity because God gave us the privilege of being made in his image.

Christians still have to talk about a certain kind of freedom too. It is not that we can do whatever we want. That is too simple a definition of freedom. We are free in relationship to God. We make "free choices" to accept or reject God and his divine law. If a person steals, kills or commits adultery, he or she must expect the divine law to declare him guilty. He is not excused because of "contingencies." He simply *must not transgress*, under pressure of all the contingencies in the world, or *he is guilty*.

Scriptural revelation is higher than natural contingencies. Spiritual aid, powerful spiritual aid, comes through that revelation. The powers of God are stronger than any natural pressures. Divine assistance is reliably available for the asking.

The Holy Spirit is more than doctrine in this battle. He provides a means for living above the pressure of contingencies. It is no accident with God that the cross is the central focus of the Christian world view. Looking back with admiration, we can understand the words of St. Paul who warned that we are played upon by powerful forces: we wrestle with them, he says in Ephesians. And so the cross—that powerful victory against sin and death and evil in all its forms. That victory is employed time and again in the life of every believer. Contingencies are strong and the pressure is great. We are humbled in our pride as we recognize the power of the forces massed around us. But we refuse to be their pawns.

In an age when we have gained tremendous self-knowledge, only to be equally baffled by the powerful contingencies which force their way into our lives, we need the life of the Holy Spirit. We are free to make that choice: to seek divine aid, to submit ourselves to Jesus Christ, to invite the Holy Spirit to invade our personalities and exercise his autonomy against these contingencies. Our choice is for grace and against contingency.

And yet this is one choice we cannot be "proud" of. There is no special credit for doing what we were created to do. We would have been simpletons if we had not chosen the one thing we needed most. And since through Scripture we understand that God made us, how natural and right to discover that true freedom comes in giving ourselves back to our Originator.

"It is he that hath made us, and not we ourselves," we have learned to say (Ps. 100:3 KJV). "Then what becomes of our boasting?" asks St. Paul. "It is excluded," he answers in Romans 3:27. Once we walked by nature but now by grace. Instead, now, "according to the riches of his glory he may grant you to be strengthened with might through his Spirit in the inner man" (Eph. 3:16). The Christian finds freedom there, dignity there.

With new Skinnerian self-knowledge, we may see much in our "inner contingencies" that will make us tremble and pause. The roots of our selfishness and pride may show off more clearly. We will bite our tongues and take back our proud talk. We will not want to defeat someone.

At the same time, we will refuse one thing that the behaviorists want us to understand: that we are totally victimized by whatever has gone before in our lives, that we are at the mercy of our past. True, those past incidents of pain and pleasure did become a part of our internal network somewhere. But that is not all there is to it. There is hope, redemption, healing. We are not victims.

We can be New Humans. But secular humanism, pushed to its logical extreme, is a dead end. If the Knowledge Explosion is irrevocably with us, let us welcome it. But its derivative, secular humanism, is only half-humanism, a half-truth. We are *more* than machines, and more too than individualized consciousness. We will never be content without a wider vision. Nevertheless, the challenge of the new humanism increases our respect for our Christian heritage in the purposes of God. Those new pressures which the humanist thinkers place on Christian perceptions expand and sharpen our comprehension of the dimensions of divine creaturehood.

Knowledge and Pain: Conclusion

5

The main assumption of this book has been that one should sift all knowledge for its good. It may appear that this is an easy matter and that one can emerge unscathed from the process. But the quest is never without pain—whether the pain of effort, the pain of frustration or even the pain of despair, at least for brief moments before the light breaks. For no light dawns without cost, living cost. It would be irresponsible to assume that one could breeze through the maze of modern thinking without some soul-searched hours. But the price is never too dear; the reward is light.

The problem then is to survive the pain, to prevent despair in the middle of the quest before the light comes. A first step is to realize that pain is inevitable on such a journey. The next is to identify those sources of strength that will sustain us along the way when the darkness threatens to overwhelm. What follows is a series of reminders about the difficulties of the quest and of the ways some have grappled with them and prevailed.

The Other Side of Darkness

The struggle, St. Paul reminds, is a mighty one, a struggle not just against flesh and blood but against all the powers of heaven and earth, "against the world rulers of this present darkness." During moments of darkness, this description seems telling and appropriate. But Paul suggests a spiritual armor, a "breastplate of righteousness," a "shield of faith," a "flaming sword," "the sword of the Spirit, which is the word of God." The apostle reassures us that it is God who must prevail, that the darkness must lose at last. Darkness will be overwhelmed in light, overwhelmed universally at the end of time, and in the meantime, personally, for the duration of the quest. When intellectual darkness forebodes, God's words seek to reassure.

In fact, anything which knowledge offers must be seen in that perspective, that God is the God of all truth, the Author of light. Left to itself, knowledge can produce as much suffering as the suffering it offers to relieve. New depths of human experience and insight, without God, can still yield the nightmare.

Christians know the nightmare. Many have been there. They remember the pain which vicarious imagination brought, perhaps late in the night, after reading some of the hard thinkers. It was the pain of wondering, in the stillness, if one was mistaken after all to hold out for God when the rest of the world had forgotten him. In the stillness, alone, with the realization that one is a hold-out for a God at whom sages seem to sneer, one wonders if he has lost his senses. Perhaps the believer may even try the quest alone for a while, convinced to abandon God for a time. But that seeker who has been touched by God most often discerns that the mind divorced from God becomes a new and harrowing dimension of hell.

Those who have come out of such a night wonder why mankind persists in calling itself "master of the universe, stage-director of the human process." By his own hand the creature computes the courses of the stars, the destinies of the billions of earth dwellers, and believes he has conquered. Free at last of all those shackles of superstition and religion, he congratulates himself. He intends to overcome and prevail.

Indeed, this exultation is a representative attitude among some. There is agreement, even rejoicing, that the world has come of age without God. But the rejoicing often seems to be tempered by a certain sadness, a futility, a confusion of purpose and destiny, and a consequent busyness that avoids the ultimate questions. It pains Christians to see so many turning another way.

The following words of a prominent thinker of this century, W. T. Stace, surely bring such pain to those who read sensitively.

> Those who wish to resurrect Christian dogmas are not, of course, consciously dishonest. But they have that kind of unconscious dishonesty which consists in lulling oneself with opiates and dreams. Those who talk of a new religion are merely hoping for a new opiate. Both alike refuse to face the truth that there is, in the universe outside man, no spirituality, no regard for values, no friend in the sky, no help or comfort for man of any sort. To be perfectly honest in the admission of this fact, not to seek shelter in new or old illusions, not to indulge in wishful dreams about this matter, this is the first thing we shall have to do.[1]

Hard words. Is faith but illusion? A person may at times be sorely tempted to follow such a compelling description of the modern attitude, and consequently to walk free of faith.

Against the compelling power of such a challenge, how can one respond? The problem again is recognizing interpretation. And the road to a solution is time—long moments of time to think, and to reflect. Increasingly we come to recognize interpretation when it occurs.

In the essay from which the excerpt comes, "Man against Darkness," Stace uses a great deal of "history" and "facts" to lead the reader to his goal. But the problem with such a use of facts is this: almost every fact is screened to the reader through an interpreter. And while interpretation makes data more interesting, gives it a kind of life, the interpretive process can become foe as well as friend. It makes information palatable and interesting, but it often overwhelms with its own subjectivity. This is especially true when data are offered in the guise of objectivity.

Two things are needed. First, immediate recognition of interpretation when it occurs. Second, and even more so, courage when one is so artfully wooed by the power of persuasion. We may not immediately be able to marshall the proper insights to counter the argument in a more satisfying direction. But at least we can learn to say, "This is but interpretation." That ability removes the sting.

In the morning, on the other side of the hard sayings and the saddening interpretations, Christians often find themselves instinctively reassessing and, at length, reaffirming the sources of their own convictions. "How is it that Christian beliefs came to have such overwhelming influence on my life, so much so that other views and schemes seemed inadequate before it? And how did I come to understand that the unity of faith and thought are possible? How did I come to that place where the worlds of the spirit, the mind and the material seemed compatible and at peace?"

Reflecting on these questions, we trace once again the long spaces across the long nights where the tenets of belief and the thorny precepts of life struggled against one another in the darkness. Often it was tempting to abandon the hope of a unity between faith and thought. It was tempting to "have faith only" and leave the hard questions alone.

Indeed many have paled at the attempt to bring together certain puzzling discoveries with the life of faith. Yet others have persisted, have respected the difficulties and have persevered. These were determined to keep the life of faith and thought as close together as possible, while fully aware of the limitations of human understanding. A clear-headed view of one's limitations is essential and healthy. But a consequent faith in the resources of God to make the unity possible, even in some measure, urges us on despite the inevitable restrictions.

Pressing on we find reward. We come to understand theological truth as something other than mere dogma. We begin to perceive those intimate connections between Christian theology and the life we live. Through observation and personal trial, we become convicted of the validity of the Bible. Through the testing of time we find it a reliable touchstone at innumerable crises of life and faith. It has daily served us in personal, social and ethical decisions. It has not disappointed or deceived; instead it has seemed increasingly broad, complete, adequate for the severest complexity which life has offered. In these many respects we have come to regard the biblical record as a comprehensive compilation of wisdom and of spiritual truth.

The more we see the biblical account as a reliable base, the more willing we become to test other experiences and ideas by its precepts. We find an even sanity, a respect for personhood, an undaunted realism, and, too, the possibility that restoration and redemption provide a surer foundation for goodness and idealism than the roads other thinkers have proposed. Nowhere else is there such a delicate balance between unblinking recognition of evil and commitment to human moral responsibility, such undaunted hope, such promise of goodness and restoration.

To be sure, everyone chooses some base for his thought life. Yet some bases seem more adequate than others. Testing the adequacy of Scripture through thoughtful analysis, Christians find the biblical base without equal. So, by certain key precepts found there, they weigh, judge and compare the many views of other thoughtful people.

Though one prizes biblical truth in this way, it is not necessary to use biblical truth as a shield against the words of others. We should still seek to listen and understand. The long nondogmatic ascent to an understanding of biblical truth should keep us from intentional dogmatism toward the words of others. Others have insights which contribute to our own understanding. Thus, though exposure to dissenting views may alarm, Christians should insist on hearing and understanding the thoughts of others.

The Dangers of Faith Apart from Thought

The slow and careful testing of the biblical record may cause impatience in those who came to the Bible at once, at the moment of conversion, embracing the biblical record as an act of faith. Yet even those who travel the long, careful path conclude that the record is worthy to be trusted. At their conversion they accorded it both respect and trust. But because they have also tested it day after day in the life of faith and thought, they have come to value in increasing measure its trustworthiness, its breadth and scope.

Those who embrace the doctrines of Christianity without carefully understanding them sorely limit their own effectiveness as Christians. These believers never assess and understand the Scriptures against the wider context of life. At once they begin to confine themselves within self-imposed limits they do not fully grasp. Dogma becomes a defense against many things which they do not understand and do not intend to understand. Such people have narrowed the borders of the intellectual life so hazardously that they live thereafter in isolation and ineffectualness. Should an intellectual challenge penetrate their defenses, their whole faith could collapse.

A different danger awaits those who maintain an active and vigorous intellectual life which functions independently of their commitment to Christ. Within the soul, they know they have "come home." They entertain no further doubt of that and are at peace. But their mind is uninvolved in the transformation. This could be due to long years of training under another interpretive system (whether relativism, a partial idealism or hard realism) or to a fear of the difficulties of including the mind in the transformation. Seeing no way to correlate the contents of the thought life with the new understandings of belief, they prefer to keep the cognitive realms of life separate from the spiritual. This is often the case with those whose discipline is intensely specialized. Somehow the more specialized the discipline, the easier it is to maintain the dichotomy, to maintain the conviction that the two worlds simply do not, need not, touch each other. Some view such correlation as a hopeless task and abandon it altogether, living in two worlds at once.

Still others come farther, even halfway. Then recognizing the problems in pressing toward a unity, they establish a truce after only approaching the goal. Once meeting a point of conflict, these seekers choose to quit the quest.

There are others who press on, more slowly, to a compatability between the two realms. These last come, in time, to see the Bible through the eyes of the intellect as well as the heart, to respect in ever-increasing measure the breadth of its provision, and to survey their intellectual apprehensions by its light. It is this last estate that offers the greatest rewards to those who are not put off by temporary pain, temporary intellectual distress.

Promises of Understanding

Clearly what is not recommended is any form of dogmatism which would blunt or pervert the progress of legitimate questions when they seem to be incompatible with Christian precepts. Instead, even if pain threatens, Christians should fully consider and understand such challenges, turning them from side to side to see what new angles of perception and insight might be there. Trusting that the final conclusions will be compatible with the perceptions of faith, we need not hurry to make them so, to force them unnaturally to yield. Otherwise we might miss something important that careful examination offers. Slow, careful, unthreatened thought is the hallmark of the process. If a perception appears to be good at first appraisal and later proves to be fraught with problems, the incompatibilities will become apparent with time, just as an ill-advised friendship slowly produces its own inherent difficulties. Time is a boon. Haste blunts the understanding and has little else to recommend it. Christians trust God for the intellect and believe that the intellectual process is sufficiently valid to produce some degree of understanding. Though we understand our finiteness and our proneness to error, we value the mind highly among the endowments of a creature of God.

True, there are dangers for those who would unite faith and thought. True, there is pain and anguish for those who would understand the views of those holding different perspectives. But beyond the pain, beyond the danger, lies a highly prized goal: the stretching of the mind to perceive the works of God. Beyond the pain and the pitfalls stands an intense and deeply founded determination to persist in the life of inquiry.

This determination is not always well understood. To some, the motivation for reading, investigating, thinking is primarily to ward off the threats and indignities which God has suffered in this age. Alas, it would take a specialist to adequately defend God on intellectual grounds. Most feel unequal to the task. (Some even question whether God needs such defense; perhaps he can take care of his own defense, ultimately.)

Others claim an offensive posture: we should read to be better ambassadors of the faith. We read not just to defend God but also to present God, to show by knowledge and understanding where others have gone wrong that some may be assisted to go right. This is a more admirable motivation, far more positive and good. There are many errors to correct in this world. If one can correct a few, and thereby win believers, so much to the good. But after one has rebuked error, what then? One must go on to build.

Hence, a third alternative must be understood to govern the venture of thought. God created us for essentially positive purposes. After the Fall, negative elements became a part of the picture as well. But God's original purposes have not been completely clouded. We are fallen now, broken, but still in the image of God. We are now involved in a work of restoration and creation, of discovering again what it is to be made in that image. This is the higher rationale which governs the quest of Christian thinkers.

Made in the image of God: an awesome concept. God formed Adam out of the dust of the ground and then, yes, and then, he breathed into him the breath of life. More than the dust of the ground; possessor of the breath of life. God breathed the breath of life and Adam became a living soul. Made in the image of God. A living soul.

How, then, to be that living soul, to be what God intended? Since the Fall there have come, in sequence, atonement, redemption, regeneration. And through these it is possible again, as before the Fall, to claim the legacy to be that living soul, made in the image of God.

Hence, the mind, the mental powers, the ability to speculate, to perceive, to wonder, to understand God as truth. And they that worship him must worship him in spirit and in truth. Consider the implications of the word *worship*: to wonder, to speculate, to commune, to understand. It is written, "Everything that I learned from my Father I have made known to you" (Jn. 15:15 NIV). Everything. Unlimited possibilities of insight, understanding, perception. "Let the word of Christ dwell in you richly as you teach and counsel one another with all wisdom" (Col. 3:16 NIV).

How is it that these promises of understanding are offered? How can God promise such things to his creatures? Because he bestowed on us, as his image-bearing creatures, the very capacity to understand and comprehend such things. True, it is the Holy Spirit, God's awesome gift to the redeemed, who activates this understanding, which gives strength, nerve and sinew to it. But the Holy Spirit activates what is there, the mind, the understanding, the insight, the intellectual equipment which God originally bestowed at creation.

Therefore, "whatever is true, whatever is honorable, whatever is just, whatever is pure, whatever is lovely, whatever is gracious, if there is any excellence, if there is anything worthy of praise, think about these things" (Phil. 4:8). Any excellence. Anything worthy of praise.

Is there something in the work of everyone that is worthy of praise? All who draw the breath of life inherit the resources of creation. In every work there is likely to be some virtue, some lesson, some newness, whatever the interpretive mold. The record says, he makes his sun to shine upon the just and the unjust. So too does knowledge and insight in some degree come to all. The quality of the gift may vary. The degree of insight and contribution may vary. But there will be something of worth. So, if there be anything of good, of newness, of contribution in a thinker's work, one should "think about these things." That is the point of this book—that we may welcome and discern what is good.

Of course, all hard thinking brings pain as well as insight, darkness as well as light. But the light gained from the effort is worth the pain of the quest. Seeing more clearly into a sequestered corner of the creation, following hard upon a discoverer's thoughts until we see and hear what he sees and hears, we will find the rewards irrevocable. "What hath God wrought?" declared Alexander Graham Bell, hearing the voice in the small speaker which he held in his hand. What he meant was, how is the universe so constructed that a voice may carry across such distances? By studying the physics of the telephone one sees as he did the awesome extensions of knowledge and possibility. "What hath God wrought!" It is enough to see farther than before. To see the extended frontiers, the unlimited prospects of discovery within God's creation. For Christians, seeing turns at once to worship.

Whenever we come upon a thinker-discoverer who believes his insights disprove the Author of possibility and knowledge, so much is our pain increased. But Christians need not accept the agnostic supposition which accompanies the insight, even while admiring it. The process of sifting, weighing, gleaning never ends. If there is any good, think on it. If there is anything incompatible with our understanding of the nature of God, creation, redemption, leave it or let it rest for another time. But under no circumstances be overpowered by it. There is no cause for that. Gullibility and despair are incompatible with the sustaining sources of the Christian mind and must be refused.

Light in the Morning

God is at work in the world in ways far beyond our power to comprehend them. We can refuse to be discouraged by evil or opposition because of that. The gospel means lifting people from salvation into a life overflowing with the fruits of redemption. Intellectual enlightenment is one of those fruits. We should be willing to look for truth in any quarter. And wherever we find purpose, order, beauty we will offer praise, as Paul told us to do.

So we avoid the spirit of fearfulness which looks only for errors and mistakes. We seek instead to understand whatever insights and intuitions another of any stripe has understood and contributed—even though we disagree with him in several ways. We respect the validity of the experiences of others and thank them for their contribution to the growing store of knowledge. We respect both thinkers and their tools. There are many ways to know, many tools, besides the ones we may have chosen to work with: the rational, the logical, the subjective, the mystical, the intuitive, the mythological, the empirical and many others all serve to light up a larger whole. No one method will ever stand alone. None should demand to. But none deserves to be rejected, either. As redeemed seekers we learn not to condemn too easily. We learn instead to appreciate and to say so.

So we press on, astutely, carefully but confident of this: God made us thinking creatures; somehow it is our mandate, it is what God wants, to seek hard after understanding and insight, to endure the pain of the quest, and to expect light in the morning.

For Further Thought

Becker, Carl. "Climates of Opinion" in Heavenly City of the Eighteenth-Century Philosophers. *New Haven: Yale University Press, 1932.*

Bell, Daniel. The Coming of Post-Industrial Society. *New York: Basic Books, 1973.*

Boulding, Kenneth. The Meaning of the Twentieth Century. *New York: Harper, 1964, 1965.*

Eiseley, Loren. The Immense Journey. *New York: Vintage Books, 1946, 1957.*

Hughes, Robert. "The Cosmos Is a Giant Thought." Horizon, *XVI, no. 1, Winter 1974, pp. 4-21.*

Huxley, Aldous. Brave New World and Brave New World Revisited. *New York: Harper, 1960.*

Huxley, Julian. Religion without Revelation. *New York: Harper, 1927, 1957.*

Joad, C. E. M. The Present and Future of Religion. *New York: Macmillan, 1930.*

Krutch, Joseph Wood. The Best of Two Worlds. *New York: Wm. Sloane Assoc., 1953.*

_____________. If You Don't Mind My Saying So: Essays on Man and Nature. *New York: Wm. Sloane Assoc., 1964.*

_____________. *"The Mystique of the Desert" from* The Voice of the Desert. *Reprinted in* Ten Contemporary Thinkers, *ed. V. Amend and L. Hendricks, Glencoe, IL: Free Press, 1964.*

Monod, Jacques. Chance and Necessity. *New York: A. Knopf, 1971.*

Orwell, George. 1984. *New York: Harcourt Brace, 1949.*

Planck, Max. "The Meaning and Limits of Exact Science" in Scientific Autobiography and Other Writings. *New York: Philosophical Library, 1949.*

Potter, Van Rennsselaer. Bioethics: The Bridge to the Future. *Englewood Cliffs, NJ: Prentice Hall, 1971.*

Reich, Charles A. The Greening of America. *New York: Bantam, 1970.*

Russell, Bertrand. "A Free Man's Worship" in Mysticism and Logic. *2nd ed. Scranton, PA: Barnes and Noble, 1954.*

Skinner, Burrhus Frederick. Beyond Freedom and Dignity. *New York: A. Knopf, 1971.*

_____________. Walden II. *New York: Macmillan, 1948, 1963.*

Stace, W. T. "Man against Darkness." Atlantic Monthly, *182, Sept. 1948, 53-58.*

Thoreau, Henry David. Walden *and "Walking" in* The Portable Thoreau. *New York: Viking Press, 1947, 1962, 1964.*

Whitehead, Alfred North. Science and the Modern World. *New York: Macmillan, 1926.*

Notes

Chapter 2

[1]Carl Becker, "Climates of Opinion," *Heavenly City of the Eighteenth-Century Philosophers* (New Haven: Yale University Press, 1932).

[2]Alfred North Whitehead, *Science and the Modern World* (New York: Macmillan, 1926), p. 185.

[3]Max Planck, "The Meaning and Limits of Exact Science," *Scientific Autobiography and Other Writings* (New York: Philosophical Library, 1949), pp. 81-82.

[4]Ibid., p. 117.

[5]Robert Hughes, "The Cosmos Is a Giant Thought," *Horizon*, Jan. 1974, pp. 4-21.

[6]Planck, "Religion and Natural Science," *Scientific Autobiography*, p. 184.

[7]Ibid., p. 177.

[8]Ibid., p. 187.

[9]Ibid., p. 186.

[10]Ibid., p. 156.

[11]Jacques Monod, *Chance and Necessity* (New York: A. Knopf, 1971), p. 180.

[12]Ibid.

[13]Ibid.

[14]Ibid., p. 173.

Chapter 3

[1]Henry David Thoreau, "Walking," in *The Portable Thoreau* (New York: Viking Press, 1947, 1964), p. 602.

[2]Ibid., "Spring," p. 543.

[3]Ibid., "Baker Farm," p. 449.

[4]Joseph Wood Krutch, "The Mystique of the Desert," *The Voice of the Desert* (1935), reprinted in V. E. Amend & L. Hendrick, eds., *Ten Contemporary Thinkers*, (Glencoe, IL: Free Press, 1964), p. 157.

[5]Joseph Wood Krutch, *If You Don't Mind My Saying So: Essays on Man and Nature*, "XIII" (New York: William Sloane Assoc., 1964), pp. 400-02.

[6]Loren Eiseley, *The Immense Journey* (New York: Vintage Books, 1946, 1957), p. 204.

[7]Ibid., p. 210.

Chapter 4

[1]Julian Huxley, "Evolutionary Humanism," *Religion without Revelation* (New York: Harper, 1927, 1957), pp. 181-212.

[2]Huxley, "Developed Religion," *Religion without Revelation*, pp. 165-80.

Chapter 5

[1]W. T. Stace, "Man against Darkness," *Atlantic Monthly*, Sept. 1948, pp. 53-58.